Mt.
St. H

A Sleeping
Volcano
Awakes

Mount St. Helens

A Sleeping Volcano Awakes

Marian T. Place

ILLUSTRATED WITH PHOTOGRAPHS

DODD, MEAD & COMPANY, NEW YORK

FRONTISPIECE:

Aerial view of Mount St. Helens during height of major eruption on Sunday, May 18, 1980. U.S. Geological Survey

Map on page 58 and diagram on page 11 are by Dyno Lowenstein

1   2   3   4   5   6   7   8   9   10

Library of Congress Cataloging in Publication Data

Place, Marian T. (Marian Templeton), date
    Mount St. Helens: a sleeping volcano awakes.

    Includes index.
    Summary: Discusses the 1980 eruptions of Mount Saint
Helens, one of the active volcanoes that rings the
Pacific Ocean.
    1. Saint Helens, Mount (Wash.)—Juvenile literature.
[1. Saint Helens, Mount (Wash.)   2. Volcanoes]   I.   Title.
QE523.S23P54   979.7'8419   81–43222
ISBN 0–396–07976–8   AACR2

To
Sara Saam

Contents

Introduction

Volcanoes remind me of tigers. Asleep, both are handsome and appear to be harmless, even tame. Aroused from slumber, they can be playful and entertaining, or treacherous and wildly dangerous. When either begins to twitch and waken, it helps a lot if you know what can happen and act accordingly.

Fortunately, very few of us come face-to-face with a live tiger except across a wide moat in a zoo or through the iron bars of a circus cage. Thus, tigers really aren't a problem for us. Neither are most volcanoes which are far, far away and sleep so long, hundreds or thousands of years, that we rarely think about them.

Recently, however, we Americans discovered that a very

active and periodically violent volcano loomed in our continental backyard. So that is what this book describes . . . Mount St. Helens, in the state of Washington, which erupted May 18, 1980, with a destructive wallop equal to that of a 10-megaton hydrogen bomb.

Between then and February, 1981, there were five more less-violent outbursts. Scientists cannot predict how many more eruptions may occur before the exhausted volcano becomes dormant, or inactive, and no longer poses a threat to people, wildlife, forests, streams, fish, crops, insects, the air we breathe, the Pacific Northwest.

Meantime how do we live with a tigerish volcano in our midst? We plan, that's how. First, the volcano teaches scientists and engineers and ordinary people how a *live* volcano really behaves. Then they teach us, and after we do our homework, we plan how to cope today, tomorrow, and in the future.

Why bother planning?

Here is a brief description of what Mount St. Helens did on May 18. Its catastrophic explosion blasted 98,000 cubic feet of rock, ice, and ash into the sky, lowering the 9,677-foot-high summit by 1,313 feet. The present elevation is 8,364 feet. After months of studies of the devastated slopes, U.S. Geological Survey volcanologists reported the total material ejected measured 143,500 cubic feet, nearly as much as entombed the Italian village of Pompeii when Mount Vesuvius erupted in A.D. 79. Mount St. Helens also triggered gigantic mudslides that bright Sunday morning and searing pyroclastic flows which destroyed well over a hundred thousand acres of prime timberland, recreation parks, homes, roads, and bridges. The official count of casualties now lists 31 known dead and 30 missing-and-presumed-dead, a figure that will change as more bodies are found and one or more listed as missing later make an appearance. The eruption also dropped tons of volcanic ash onto the states of Washington, Idaho, and Montana, wreaking billions of dollars of damage. High-altitude winds sped some ash across the nation and even around the world.

While there are active volcanoes in Alaska and Hawaii, Mount St. Helens was not the first to erupt within the continental boundaries of the United States, nor will it be the last. Today few readers realize that Mount Lassen in northern California erupted in 1914 and 1915 before simmering down in 1917. It is still dormant. Mount Lassen and Mount St. Helens are only two of a chain of magnificent snow-capped volcanoes soaring at approximately 45-to-80-mile intervals on a north-south line along the crest of the Cascade Mountains, only 100 miles inland from the Pacific Ocean. There are other stately volcanic peaks in that chain: Lassen and Shasta in California; McLoughlin, Crater Lake (the caldera of Mount Mazama), Thielsen, Bachelor, Three Sisters, Jefferson, and Hood in Oregon; Adams, St. Helens, Rainier, Glacier, and Baker in Washington; and Mount Garibaldi in British Colum-

MOUNT ST. HELENS

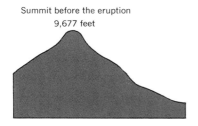

Summit before the eruption
9,677 feet

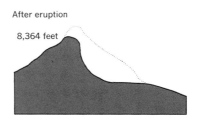

After eruption

8,364 feet

bia, Canada. All are part of a circle of active volcanoes surrounding the Pacific Ocean and known as the "Ring of Fire."

You probably would like to ask, "If Lassen and St. Helens have erupted, which one will be next?"

Take your pick. Mount Baker almost erupted five years ago. Mount Rainier has warm caves atop its highest slopes. Mount Hood has vented steam for years. Scientists agree that since the Cascade Range is geologically active, these three and others have the potential to erupt.

"When?" you ask nervously.

No one can predict the day, month, year, or century. But don't worry. Volcanoes give many warnings before they erupt. Mount St. Helens did, as you will read. From the very first tremor that hinted it was stirring from a 123-year-long dormant period, intensive studies were begun to record and interpret every clue. Overnight Mount St. Helens became a *living laboratory,* its slopes bristling with seismographs, tiltmeters, remote control cameras, and a host of other instruments. A small army of highly skilled specialists—geologists, geophysicists, volcanologists and their assistants—rode four-wheelers or helicopters in order to comb the slopes and crater for information.

While modern men created the hydrogen bomb, they have it in their power to decide when and where it can explode. But no one man, no corps of scientists or engineers, no politicians, no army of environmentalists, no governments can control the actions of aroused volcanoes. In one destructive flash they can wreak more pollution and devastation than anything man designs. Obviously we must learn to cope with these handsome deadly creations of nature if present and future generations are to live safely and happily alongside the volcanoes in the western United States. Hopefully, Mount St. Helens will teach us how to accomplish this.

Remember, generations have lived and still live close by them without fear. Rainier, St. Helens, Hood, Bachelor, Shasta, and others attract hundreds of thousands of hunters, hikers, fishermen, skiers, boaters, and loggers onto their slopes. Portland, Oregon, flourishes with a volcano within view from its city limits. Already four-footed and winged creatures are returning slowly to the lower slopes and forests surrounding Mount St. Helens. Once more families are picnicking, berry picking, bird watching, and clicking cameras within its *safe* recreation areas. Loggers are harvesting timber, even inside the boundaries of the "red" or danger zone closest to the crater. They can carry on because they are in constant radio communication with those monitoring the peak, and know their evacuation procedures well. So do the scientists who work daily, when conditions permit, on the upper slopes and *inside* the awesome new crater. Thousands of sightseers throng the new observation centers provided by the U.S. Forest Service so that the volcano's fitful steaming and erupting can be observed safely.

For those who live in the Pacific Northwest with Mount St. Helens practically in the backyard or on the distant horizon, the volcano remains a wondrous creation to be admired and respected, not feared. We are learning to accommodate our lifestyles to this live volcano in our midst. Come see for yourselves.

—M. T. P.
Bend, Oregon

1.

Fair Warnings

Vancouver! Vancouver! This is it!"

The excited message heralding a destructive volcano eruption was shouted at 8:32 A.M. on a bright Sunday morning, May 18, 1980, by Dr. David Johnston, thirty, a volcanologist intensely involved for weeks in monitoring Mount St. Helens, 95 miles south of Seattle, Washington, and only 50 miles northeast of Portland, Oregon.

From his observation post five miles below the snow-covered summit, he felt strong earthquakes one minute apart and then, awe-stricken, watched as the entire north face of the mountain blew out laterally and an enormous jet of steam and pulverized rock rocketed skyward from the volcano's crater. As the superheated column of black smoke rose 60,000 feet—similar to the aftermath of an atomic bomb explosion—bolts of lightning, recorded at six per minute, crackled, and flaming cinders rained down on timbered slopes, setting over 300 forest fires. In an instant the 9,677-foot-high peak was reduced by 1,313 feet and its crater laid back a mile in width. From a horseshoe-shaped notch on the north rim, wave after wave of *pyroclastic flow*—not lava but a combination of searing ash-water-and-gas—hurtled 200 miles per hour down the mountainside. It obliterated or buried everything in its path, snapping off spruce and pine trees like matchsticks and toppling them like dominoes. It turned icy Spirit Lake into a cauldron of boiling mud and debris. As hot gases melted the deep snow and ice on the ski slopes, gigantic mudslides overran the North and South Forks of the Toutle River drainage, choking streams, burying roads, bridges, logging camps, machinery, dwellings, vehicles, wildlife, livestock, and human beings.

Dr. Johnston radioed the news of the initial blast from his observation post to the U.S. Geological Survey headquarters' dispatch center in the Federal Building complex at Vancouver, Washington, 45 miles southwest. At the same moment the needle on the seismograph installed at timberline 5,000 feet up the peak's west slope—and on similar instruments at the University of Washington in Seattle, the USGS (U.S. Geological Survey) observatory at Newport, the National Earthquake Center in Boulder, Colorado, and Oregon State University at Corvallis—recorded heavy zigzag marks on the graphed paper.

However, at this crucial moment only the voice of Dr. Johnston was heard. Since his arrival in late March from Menlo Park, California, the genial bearded bachelor, a field volcanol-

15

ogist for the USGS, had camped frequently at observation post Timberline Camp, 4,500 feet up the quivering north slope. His primary responsibility was to monitor an instrument pointed at the crater which analyzed gases being emitted and report changes recorded on several sensing devices. He discounted the danger of his precarious location, assuring reporters, "This is the chance of a lifetime!"

His lifetime, he should have added, since although Mount St. Helens was known to have erupted in centuries past, it was at this moment the only *live* volcano within the continental boundaries of the United States. The fact that its snorting and erupting could be seen from surrounding communities and from Portland's West Hills, and its lower slopes were easily accessible by car, had drawn thousands of sightseers, all hoping for a close-up view of a spectacular explosion.

Volcanoes do not erupt without giving fair warning, but not until sensitive modern instruments were invented could their first stirrings be noted accurately. Thus, it was 3:45 P.M. Thursday, March 20, when a moderate tremor, registering 4.1 on the Richter intensity scale, was recorded on regional seismographs. Within minutes the staff at the Forest Service headquarters received a call from Forest Ranger Charles Tonn at Spirit Lake, Washington, stating the tremor had been felt along the north base of Mount St. Helens.

"Probably nothing to worry about," he was told. It was merely an indication of the normal on-going shifting of the earth's crust. Fifty thousand or more quakes occurred yearly along the Cascade Range, but few were newsworthy.

However, Ranger Tonn recalled reading a dire prediction published in a USGS bulletin only two years before. Following exhaustive studies by Dwight R. Crandell and Donal R. Mullineaux, experienced volcanologists whom he knew, they stated that Mount St. Helens was an especially dangerous volcano and future eruptions were a certainty. Ranger Tonn couldn't help being concerned because he was the administrative officer of a large district encompassing Mount St. Helens in the Gifford Pinchot National Forest. Privately he hoped the long-dormant volcano had merely twitched and gone back to sleep.

Unfortunately for his peace of mind, multiple tremors of mild to moderate intensity, called microquakes, occurred on March 21 and 22. Seismologists and geophysicists from the USGS and the University of Washington rushed to install multiple earthquake measuring devices on the volcano's flanks. Research and experience had taught them to be conservative in their predictions, so even among their associates they could not hazard a guess whether or not St. Helens, or the "Sleeping Beauty," as many called the peak, would spring to life as a raging tiger, and when.

On March 21 Steven Malone, Craig Weaver, and Elliott Endo, University of Washington geophysicists, were monitoring newly installed instruments on the shore of Spirit Lake, whose deep cold water, 3,200-feet-high on the north slope, mirrored the snowy peak. So many tremors were being registered that they could not separate them on the graph paper. The next morning they called Donal Mullineaux in Boulder and excitedly described the mountain as "shaking like a mound of jelly," with as many as forty quakes an hour. Dr. Mullineaux and his co-author associate Dwight Crandell immediately flew to Vancouver to coordinate the scientific studies already under way.

Strange as it may seem, little documented facts about *active* volcanoes are known when compared to the wealth of studies of historic eruptions throughout the world, such as Mount Vesuvius (A.D. 79) in Italy, Krakatoa (1883) in Indonesia, Mount Mazama in southernmost Oregon (4600 B.C.), and in more recent times Mount Lassen (1914–1917) in California and Mount Mezyianny (1956) in the Soviet Union. Small wonder, then, that as information on St. Helens was released to news media, scientists in North America and the world descended on the small city of Vancouver. One of these was Dr. David Johnston. Now the word was out among these specialists who relied on seismograph reports, not hearsay or news bulletins, that a big show starring St. Helens could be brewing. While they speculated freely among themselves, publicly they curbed their tongues for fear of triggering panic among hundreds of loggers and residents of small communities nearby. The latter were feeling the tremors, yet few believed *their* peak was going to blow. Still, the prospect made lively conversation. Inevitably, word leaked out to radio, television, and newspaper reporters, so that by Tuesday, March 25, Mount St. Helens was very much in the news. To their credit, they also were cautious, not wanting to alarm people nor look silly by forecasting dire behavior of a peak that so far failed to produce a puff of steam, let alone burning lava. Maybe the "old girl" would prove to be a dud.

Loggers and log truck haulers, a highly independent, self-reliant group, thought the excitement was hogwash. Meantime Ranger Tonn and other Forest Service personnel and their families residing in the Gifford Pinchot National Forest areas surrounding the peak were advised that evacuation might be imminent. But when newsmen asked Harry Truman, eighty-three, who had operated a small guest lodge on the shore of Spirit Lake for fifty-three years, "Do you plan to evacuate?"

the crusty oldster snorted, "Heck, no, I ain't leavin'. Some o' them shocks darned near shook my socks off, but I ain't leavin'." His show of defiance made the old man a media hero overnight.

However, the scientists had the advantage over the local folk. From their studies they knew that violent eruptions resulting in indescribable destruction had occurred in the past from the vents, or throats, of Mount St. Helens and neighboring Mount Adams, 35 miles to the east, Mount Hood 60 miles southeast in Oregon, and Mount Lassen in California. The studies also indicate that the most awesome eruption in the West occurred when 16,000-foot-high Mount Mazama, 225 miles south of Mount St. Helens, blew its top, creating deep and intensely blue Crater Lake.

One week after the first tremor, at 12:36 P.M. Thursday, March 27, St. Helens boomed and then spat a plume of steam and ash that rose 10,000 feet in the air. Mike Beard, aloft in Portland television station KGW's traffic report plane, suddenly shouted, "This thing is erupting! Mount St. Helens is erupting!" Instantly his words were transmitted by teletype machines to news media worldwide. Beard witnessed a good show as hot gases, rising from roiling magma far below, shot ash and steam skyward. First aloft to photograph the phenomena was a news team from *The Columbian,* published at Vancouver, Washington. Exposures were obtained of a large cavity 250 feet in diameter and 150 feet deep in the snowy summit, its edges now blackened with ash. There were also several mile-long fissures gaping on the north slope for three miles downward. One tremor registering 4.5 was clocked at 2:00 P.M. and eight more before dark.

Now the big question was whether the volcano would poke

along at this level of activity for months, or whether it was speeding toward a record-breaking eruption. Geologists partially answered the question by saying, "The volcano is entering a new phase." Phase One, the curtain raiser, was over and Phase Two was now under way.

Until March 27 Forest Service press briefings originated from a "volcano emergency communications center" at the Gifford Pinchot National Forest headquarters in Vancouver. As hordes besieged the center with queries and telephones jangled day and night, the staff was overwhelmed. Foresters are not geologists and could not be expected to provide in-depth scientific information.

When Geological Survey personnel flocked to the scene, cooperation between the two federal agencies became urgent. Two portable office buildings were set up adjoining the forest headquarters to provide work space for Geological Survey people and their sophisticated equipment. Also added was a scientific information dispatch center, with radio communication with specialists and instruments working on the volcano and in the airways above. It issued only data on the volcano's behavior. Now, through two information centers, the Forest Service and Geological Survey spoke for themselves, employing their own aircraft, pilots, and photographers to gather information to meet their needs. The incredibly complex administrative problems resulting from the eruptions remained the province of the Forest Service.

Although St. Helens and several adjoining volcanoes are about a million years old, it is the youngest in geological time. Since 400 B.C. St. Helens alternated long dormant periods within months of violent eruptions. It might not be as large as others around the globe, nor as destructive—before May

18—but it possessed a peculiarity others did not. Core drilling revealed that it was made up of alternating layers of unstable ash and lava which concealed the base of a still older volcano 37,000 years old. When prehistoric men inched their way across the Bering Strait land base exposed during the last Ice Age and hunted their way southward through present Washington, repeated eruptions of lava, cooling and building layer upon layer, buried the old core and built St. Helens up to its 9,677-foot-high elevation. The uppermost portion of the modern cone developed only 400 years ago!

Around 1800 this "strato" or layered volcano broke a 150-year-long dormant period with an enormous eruption of pumice. Activity continued off and on through the 1830s and 1840s, with the last eruptive period ending in 1857.

No doubt about it. Phase Two of its present active period would produce some surprises.

2.

The Big Bang

During the last week in March and in early April a number of residents at Spirit Lake and along State Highway 504 and the Clark-Skamania county line evacuated their homes. While many viewers were excited at having a smoking volcano in their midst, the scientists remained deeply worried. Their greatest concern was that the heat and force of a major eruption would create huge mudslides which would overwhelm a chain of Pacific Power & Light Company reservoirs along the Lewis River, twelve miles to the south, collapsing dams and flooding ranches, summer homes, and extensive recreational campgrounds. As a precaution the utility company ordered the levels of the reservoirs lowered thirty feet. Fishermen, boaters, and water skiers complained loudly, but in vain. It seemed as if any person inconvenienced by the well-meant precautions of any agency put as much flack in the air as St. Helens spewed ash.

Mindful of danger from avalanches, the Forest Service declared the mountain off-limits to skiers and snowshoers. Also, officials of various local, county, and state law enforcement and emergency planning agencies hastily assembled to devise plans for an orderly evacuation of possible danger areas, those within 20 miles of the volcano. Already, traffic problems had developed on Highway 504 from the I-5 freeway at Castle Rock to Spirit Lake, and along the forks of the Toutle River, as sightseers crowded vantage points, hoping to be present at the magic moment when Mount St. Helens blew its top. The March 27 outburst was thought of as a rehearsal for the main event.

Those who camped overnight on March 28 atop 3,926-foot-high Mitchell Peak were wakened about 2:00 A.M. by a loud boom and whistling sounds. In the brilliant moonlight they watched a great plume of steam rise from the crater. Another eruption at 3:45 A.M. blew ash three miles into the sky and was followed by three quakes registering 4.0 on the Richter intensity scale. Later observers learned the volcano had blown out a second crater. Three small mudflows, not lava, dribbled a thousand feet down the slope. The east and south slopes turned gray from the ash projected by gases roiling from magma far below the surface.

Starting at dawn that day, the Forest Service and Geological Survey communications centers were overwhelmed with telephone calls from out-of-state news media. By late afternoon well-dressed, self-assured reporters representing *The New York Times,* the Los Angeles *Times,* the National Geographic

Society, the Smithsonian Institution, the *Washington Post,* and others, flew in, as did reporters from other major newspapers and television stations across the country and throughout the West. So great was the need for telephones that a mobile trailer was moved onto the Federal Building complex and nine pay telephones hooked up. Camera crews from far and wide, amateur and professional, swamped local aviation firms with requests for aerial survey flights. Federal Aviation Administration authorities had to monitor a crazy merry-go-round of flights over and around the peak. Attempts to enforce a "no flights within five miles" were futile. Pilots flew closer and closer, and at least one helicopter landed on the rim so its foolhardy passengers could climb down into the crater to take photographs! An advisory roadblock warning the public to turn back was placed at Camp Baker on Highway 504, but proved ineffective. Hundreds of drivers, cyclists, and hikers ignored it.

At Vancouver, Longview, and small hamlets such as Cougar, Yale, Camas, and Castle Rock, merchants and street vendors enjoyed a brisk business selling T-shirts lettered "Ski Mount St. Helens" and portraying a skier outracing burning lava. Bumper stickers read "Excuse My Ash" and "Get Your Ash Together." Stores featured the Mount St. Helens Float (root beer and ice cream) and Volcano Bar (chocolate-coated ice cream), and restaurants a Volcanoburger. Motel and sightseeing flight operators boosted their prices, profiting from the situation.

Meanwhile, newsmen and volcano watchers exhausted the Forest Service and Geological Survey personnel with persistent, impatient queries as to *when* the big eruption would occur. It was useless to tell them that restless volcanoes do not set their eruptions to accommodate press or television deadlines. Obviously, able persons familiar with volcanic studies were needed to coordinate the flood of news and queries and hold as many press conferences daily as needed. Tim Hait spoke for the Geological Survey, while the Forest Service summoned Terry Virgin from his duties as director of the million-visitor Lava Lands Visitors Center in Oregon's Deschutes National Forest. But frustration mounted as a storm front moved in from the Pacific Ocean and the fretting volcano disappeared from view.

Finally, on Sunday morning, March 30, the skies cleared shortly before Lawelatla, as the local Cowlitz Indians called the "fire mountain," staged a truly spectacular eruption. Black ash whirled skyward for twenty minutes before drifting slowly in a southeasterly direction. Immediately barriers 10 miles west and 20 miles east of the volcano were placed across all access roads. Over 300 loggers employed by the Weyerhaeuser Company and their families were evacuated from camps on the northwest slope. Nearly forty Forest Service personnel and their families at the Mount St. Helens ranger district headquarters, twelve miles southeast of the peak, also departed immediately and established themselves at the Chelatchie Prairie Work Center, a safe 35 miles from the crater.

Pilots were warned that flying closer than five miles would earn them a stiff fine, and a command plane chartered by the USGS, circled high above, regulating air traffic. On the ground USGS crews set in place more sensors and communication links with the combined University of Washington-USGS seismographic center. Now the graph charts on these instruments were inked almost solidly black from recording tremors, which experts figured were occurring a mere half-mile below sea level, directly underneath the crater. NASA, the National Aeronautics and Space Administration, scheduled U-2 high-altitude "spy" watches to chart any changes on the skittish summit and quivering slopes.

In spite of these efforts, the I-5 freeway between Portland and Seattle and all state roads leading toward the volcano or high ground overlooking it were jammed bumper-to-bumper with volcano watchers, a good number being Canadians. News reports stated that small amounts of volcanic ash had fallen on communities along the Columbia River gorge, south of the volcano, and even on Mount Jefferson, 90 airline miles farther south in Oregon. St. Helens seemed to be in a hurry, a worrisome situation for Clark, Cowlitz, and Skamania county sheriffs' forces and evacuation coordinators. While they had been assured that lava flows usually advanced slowly enough so an orderly withdrawal of people in its path could be carried out, nearly all roads involved were jammed with sightseers.

More evidence that deadly forces were building occurred April 1 when two earthquakes registered 4.5 and 4.7 and the largest clouds of ash yet seen hurtled from the crater. At 12:30 P.M. there was an ear-splitting explosion and heavy ash fallout to the southwest, where loggers reported ash drifting down like snow.

Next, an ominous new factor was noted. *Harmonic tremors,* those caused by lava roiling and flowing upward, were recorded between 7:40 and 7:55 P.M., and more the next day about 11:00 P.M. During harmonic tremors the ground expands and contracts constantly as fluid rises through cracks in the rocks, in contrast to quakes caused by sudden shifting which fractures rock.

On April 3 a tremor registering 4.8 and more prolonged

ash eruptions were noted. The tremor knocked oldster Harry Truman out of his favorite rocking chair and caused his antique player piano to tinkle a few notes. Clouds of ash, rocks, and blocks of ice, some thirteen feet in diameter, shot skyward and then bombarded the forest surrounding Spirit Lake and the roof of Truman's lodge. Despite pleas, he insisted, "I'm goin' to set right here and watch the show."

Some gray ash dusted the Portland-Vancouver area and the Bull Run watershed, source of Portland's water supply. Hours later reports filtered in that communities east of the peak and all the way to Spokane received a light coating. When apprised of this, Governor Dixy Lee Ray declared a state of emergency existed and called the Washington National Guard to clear the access roads.

The roadblock on Highway 504 was moved 20 miles farther back from the lake. Detours to viewpoints along the I-5 freeway were bulldozed to siphon off those who ignored safety regulations and parked on the shoulders. Yet the louder the public was warned of dangers, the more spectators flocked up access roads. They complained that the closures denied their rights "to go where we want," as did the very angry residents who found themselves cut off from their homes and businesses.

No matter that still more harmonic tremors were being registered. The 150 residents of Cougar, ten miles southwest of the volcano, relied on logging and the seasonal influx of fishermen, campers, and tourists to keep them financially afloat. They were as angry about the roadblocks as they were contemptuous of "all that silly talk" about folks maybe choking to death on volcanic ash or having their little settlement buried under lava. Every spare bed had been rented to reporters and "camera dudes." Every good viewpoint was crowded.

The locals argued forcefully about being denied their rights to come and go "as we d—n please," and were supported by loggers who found themselves unemployed because the new roadblocks denied them access to their work.

Dot Elmire's and Ron Katzer's stores were stripped of snack foods, soda pop, and beer, and the tables at the Wildwood Inn, the only cafe, jammed with reporters. None of the proprietors was about to hang a "Closed" sign and hightail it out to the big city. Shucks, people said, anybody with a good head start could outrace that lava stuff if it did come oozing down the mountain. The only good thing about the whole mess was that folks could tune in on their TVs every night and see themselves or friends being interviewed by some city feller brandishing a microphone like a two-dollar cigar. "Just fumin' around, that's all she's doin', like a ornery wife," one logger described the volcano. "She'll get over bein' mad and settle down, and the sooner the better."

Up at Spirit Lake all but two residents had left, including Stan Lee, operator of a small grocery store, and campers occupying spaces in the campground. But Harry Truman still had a neighbor. Robert Kasewater, a young Portland geologist, was permitted to remain in his A-frame cabin on the lakeshore because he had a battery-operated seismograph there and was shooting a timed series of photographs of the volcano. Since the road to the lake was paved, he kept his car readied for a quick exit and felt reasonably secure. Meanwhile, Mr. Truman, with some of his fifteen cats and six pet raccoons curled up on chairs or at his feet, told newsmen, "I ain't budgin'! Last night I propped my feet up on the windowsill and looked at that mountain. I said, 'Okay, Sister, show me what you can do.' Not a dang thing happened—or is goin' to."

Unpredictably, the volcano quieted down to such an extent that some were certain it was going back to sleep. Loggers and residents clamored so to return to work or to their homes that they were given permission, providing they signed statements that they recognized the danger and would be responsible for their own safety. During the lull Dr. Johnston was airlifted by helicopter to the rim and hiked down into the crater to obtain samples of water, just as he had done previously in fretful volcanoes in Iceland and Alaska.

"Yes, it was a nerve-racking experience," he admitted later when a small crowd of newsmen was escorted to an area near timberline on the north face. "Actually, you are standing on an extremely dangerous spot. If the volcano exploded right now, we would all die. The biggest threat is not the outpouring of lava but mudflows which advance swiftly and could inundate the slopes and valley below us."

"Then you're positive there's going to be another eruption?" a reporter asked.

The fair-haired geologist, dressed like a logger, nodded. "It's already in what we call the 'throat-clearing stage.' "

"Sort of like a bomb with the fuse lighted?"

That was fairly close to the truth. The volcanologist explained that an analysis of the samples retrieved from the crater revealed that the heat source far below was made up of highly explosive material called *dacite.* That's why mudflows loomed as such a danger. For the moment, though, St. Helens behaved and everyone withdrew safely.

On his next aerial survey Dr. Johnston's trained eyes spied for the first time dim blue flames flickering at the bottom of the crater. Others, now knowing what to look for, photographed the eerie blue lights. By that time Dr. Johnston had received equipment to analyze the new phenomena and reported that the flames were caused by gas emissions related to molten lava. Next, aerial stereoscopic pictures recorded between April 7 and 12 were coupled with information from tiltmeters which measured surface changes within preset distances. The results revealed enormous forces below had slowly pushed a massive area on the north side at the head of Forsyth Glacier 320 feet upward for two miles horizontally around the north slope and .6 of a mile vertically, and also that the bottom of Spirit Lake had tilted six inches toward the volcano. Geologists interpreted such a swelling on a volcano's flank as indicating pressure was building to a massive outbreak.

St. Helens was in more of a hurry than anticipated.

In the following three weeks the volcano simmered quietly, but its north flank continued to bulge. Geologists were forced to abandon observation post Timberline Camp. Then, as the rock pushed out still farther, it chewed a 1,000-foot-deep notch in the summit wall on the north side. On May 12 a tremor registering 5.0 loosened an enormous avalanche which hurtled down the mountain at a speed of 80 miles an hour, but miraculously dribbled to a halt a quarter-mile from Spirit Lake.

However, two observation posts remained active. Coldwater I, eight miles below the summit, was a photographic observatory manned by Reid Blackburn, a meticulous twenty-seven-year-old professional on the staff of *The Columbian.* He was also under contract to furnish photographic coverage for the USGS and the National Geographic Society. He operated radio remote-controlled cameras during his long vigils.

A mile away a second observation post, Coldwater II, was manned by Dr. Johnston. A small trailer for shelter and labora-

Northeasterly side of Mount St. Helens in one of the last photographs taken prior to the May 18 eruption.

U.S. Geological Survey

Scenic view of Spirit Lake with Mount St. Helens in the background, before volcanic activity destroyed it.

Harry Truman refusing to leave his lodge at Spirit Lake.

Looking south toward Mount St. Helens across crater-pocked south shore of Spirit Lake in area where Harry Truman's lodge was located.

Mount St. Helens in action, looking east toward Mount Adams.

Trees 150 feet tall were scattered like matchsticks after the explosion. This is along the North Fork of the Toutle River.

Mudflows and fallen trees block the North Fork of the Toutle River.

Reid Blackburn, photographer for *The Columbian,* setting up remote control cameras prior to the outpouring of ash that buried him.

An informal shot of geologist David Johnston, who was first to announce the eruption with "This is it!"

David Johnston climbing down into the crater during lull in April to gather water samples for clues to the explosive quality of material being ejected from the volcano.

tory space had been airlifted onto a snowy ridge 4,000 feet above the mountain-born source of the Toutle River. Its north and south forks cascaded down through densely timbered forest where several hundred loggers and truckers worked. Scientists and sheriffs' deputies had assured logging camp superintendents that should an eruption occur, their crews had from sixty to ninety minutes to evacuate to a safe position. Rather than face layoffs, the loggers stayed on their jobs, although all cursed sightseers' vehicles still cluttering the narrow roads which should be kept clear for a safe exit. Unfortunately, the blockades had been breached by those who knew how to get around them by using unimproved logging roads. These sightseers gained little in the way of photographs because, between May 7 and 17, the peak only chuffed steam now and then or was hidden by clouds.

On Saturday, May 17, the blockade on Highway 504 was lifted for four hours so a caravan of thirty-five Spirit Lake property owners might remove valuables from their cabins. A few reporters were included in the venture. A Washington State Patrol flew over the peak, maintaining radio contact with Skamania County Sheriff Bill Closner, who led the parade. The sheriff checked on Harry Truman, who was in his usual good health and refused to leave his lodge. Bob Kasewater was also in good shape and delighted to see that friend Beverly Wetherall had brought him supplies.

The owners were shocked at the amount of volcanic ash dusting rooftops, trees, and shrubs. One woman remarked, "Everything looks like a dirty dust mop had been shaken over the area."

When it was time to leave, the owners complained that they needed more time, but the sheriff was adamant. They had to leave now. After a heated discussion he agreed to escort another caravan into the area the next morning at 10 A.M. Mollified, all except Truman, Kasewater, and Wetherall lined up their vehicles. The sheriff counted noses, started them on their way down the mountain, and took his place at the rear, making certain none stayed overnight.

That evening, the fifty-second since the first tremor, Dr. Johnston radioed from Coldwater II that in spite of moderate tremors, all was serene on the snowy heights. The next morning at 7:00 A.M. he called in his routine report, and all was quiet. But at 8:30 A.M. the ground jolted severely, and two moments later the entire north face of the volcano, a half-mile wide and a mile from top to bottom, blew out in an unexpected horizontal or lateral explosion. This was followed almost immediately by a blast and shock wave which flattened trees and other vegetation in a fan-shaped swath 8 miles long and 15 miles wide north of the peak. Finally, a gigantic plume of steam, rocks, and ice was ejected 60,000 feet into the air.

At 8:32 A.M. as Mount St. Helens erupted in full force, Dr. Johnston shouted into his radio microphone, "Vancouver! Vancouver! This is it!"

A few seconds later Dr. Johnston and Coldwater II were blown to bits.

3.

Some Witnesses' Stories

Dan LaPlaunt, seventeen, of Chehalis, Washington, isn't one to brag, but he probably knows as much about the timbered approaches to Mount St. Helens as any other teenager in the state. Even before his father, Don, a millwright foreman at the Satsop Nuclear Plant in nearby Elma, presented him with his first rifle and taught him how to use it responsibly, Dan and his two older and one younger brothers had accompanied their father on countless hunting and fishing trips. While Mr. LaPlaunt joked a lot and was good company, he made certain his boys knew how to take care of themselves in the woods, and as their arms strengthened, how to hunt with bow and arrow for deer and mountain goat. Of the four boys, Dan was the only one who liked shooting with a camera as well as with a gun.

All had followed the publicity about Mount St. Helens, and enjoyed glimpses of the smoke plumes from vantage points in Chehalis. So far, however, the LaPlaunt family had not joined the sightseers for a closer look. Dan told his father, "Everybody at school is talking about it. I feel like a jerk having to admit I haven't been up there."

"We'll go Saturday after work," his father promised. "You boys load the car."

On May 10, with the trunk of the '69 Chevrolet crammed with camping gear and grub, the family took off for a favorite campsite on a high slope above the Green River and well outside the "red zone." By late afternoon they had camp set up and Dan snapped a few exposures of the steaming peak with his Agfa camera equipped with an ordinary 50-millimeter lens. The next day he ran out of film after photographing thirty small eruptions within a four-hour period. The weather remained good and the volcano put on a pretty good show before they went home.

During the week their friends Lynn and Julie Westlund, residents of a small community near Mount Rainier, dropped by and expressed a desire for a close-up look of the volcano. Don LaPlaunt obligingly offered to direct them to the campsite. He made certain they understood it was close to a graveled logging road, just in case they had to make a quick dash down the mountain. If or when he shouted, "Run for the car!" they were to do so on the double. On Saturday, May 17, he, Dan, thirteen-year old David, and a friend, Kathy Pearson, drove up the zigzag logging road, the Westlunds following in their pickup. They arrived about midnight, unloaded, and went to sleep, the boys in the car, the Westlunds under the canopy of their pickup, and Don LaPlaunt and Kathy Pearson in sleeping bags under a tree.

Don wakened first and enjoyed his unobstructed view of the peak bathed in soft morning light. It seemed almost close enough to touch. About 8:30 A.M. a sharp tremor rattled the area, car, and pickup, waking the boys and the Westlunds. Don, watching the volcano, shouted as a puff of smoke rose from the crater, clearly visible through a saddle in a ridge between them and the peak. Dan scrambled out of his sleeping bag and stepped out of the car, focusing his camera on the column of smoke. Now roaring explosions with roiling clouds engulfed the volcano. Clouds of ash and steam, tumbling and shot through with lightning and debris, advanced toward the ridge which was only five miles from their camp. Momentarily stunned, all watched, horrified, as shock waves felled heavy timber on the volcano's slope, mowing down stout trees there and then on the ridge top.

Realizing they were directly in the path of the shock wave, Don shouted, "Run for the car! Leave everything!"

The LaPlaunts and Westlunds jumped into the Chevy and shot out of the campsite onto the road. As Don floorboarded the accelerator, taking curves at 60 miles per hour, Dan rolled down a window, leaned out, and snapped pictures. Suddenly Don spied a pickup parked alongside the road ahead, braked and shouted, "The volcano's blown its top! Get out while you can!" He tromped down on the gas pedal again and two miles farther saw campers gathered around a fire. Again he and the boys yelled, "St. Helens has erupted! Get out fast!" By this time winds of hurricane velocity roared down, snapping limbs, while lightning crackled like a string of firecrackers.

LaPlaunt streaked off, passed a clear-logged area, and approached Riffle Lake where, fortunately, a strong updraft lifted the wind force above treetop level. Don turned on the lights as darkness and flying debris overtook them. He slowed again to warn vacationers, and continued the flight. Next, mudballs pelted the car, the windshield wiper failed, and Don and David had to reach out the windows and swipe clear spots on the mud-smeared glass. By the time they leveled out, having raced fifteen miles in less than twenty minutes, the mudballs had been replaced by a blizzard of gray ash. At a junction LaPlaunt turned north, sped to the logging town of Morton, already coated with ash, then on to Onalaska where they dashed into a friend's house, called relatives in Chehalis, and bolted coffee before hurrying on home.

Everyone was still shaking when they arrived, dazed at having witnessed the most destructive eruption on the continent in modern times, and weak with relief at having escaped death. The boys and the Westlunds gave Don LaPlaunt credit for the safe flight, but he declared forcefully, "Don't thank me. Thank God."

Young David worried if the campers they warned were all right. Days later he learned some had dallied, and perished. When Kathy reported for work Monday at a Forest Service station at Packwood, forty miles northeast of Mount St. Helens, she was informed that a tree-planting crew working on the mountainside had been obliterated.

Dan had the best of it when he showed his extraordinary photographs to reporters. They promptly arranged for the best ones to be copyrighted and printed in the widely distributed Northwest Magazine section of the Sunday *Oregonian,* published June 1. One stunning photo shows the ominous boiling blast of smoke, wind, and debris approaching their campsite, another the blast wave only three miles behind the speeding car, and a third lightning striking timber close to the road.

He still hopes to return to the campsite whenever guards permit, even though it is all a wasteland now. While hundreds may forget the eruption in years to come, Dan LaPlaunt won't. He will have his own photographs to jog his memory.

The LaPlaunt experience pales before that of nineteen-year-old Roald Reitan and Venus Ann Dergan, twenty, both of Tacoma. They camped twenty miles downstream from Spirit Lake along the Toutle River. Wakened by the initial blast and follow-up roaring and crashing as a wall of water, mud, and logs catapulted down the river, they scrambled out of their sleeping bags, took one look at the rising river, and climbed atop their car. Within seconds it was engulfed and swept down a steep embankment into the river. Although Roald grabbed Venus' hand, she was tossed, screaming, into the flood. He lost sight of her several times as she bobbed up and down between the bucking logs until her head was caught between two, with only her face showing. Reitan leaped along the logs, grabbed her hair and, thanks to the bobbing motion which opened a slot, managed to pull her up until she got her feet under her. The two teetered along the logs, gasping hot acrid air and ash, spattered with scorching mudballs, and pelted with flying debris and splinters from a collapsed train trestle.

Meantime, Mike West of Rio Grande, Texas, one of the throng of sightseers who had driven, flown, biked, and hitch-hiked to Washington to see the mountain's highjinks, was standing on a bridge when he and others heard the big bang. Most dashed off to grab cameras, but as the first onslaught of a mudslide came into view, Mike heard someone shouting for help. He and a local man, Fred Winningham, started running. When they spied Roald and Venus, West told reporters later, "We grabbed onto tree limbs and tore branches and threw them down to step on in our efforts to reach them. Reitan was in pretty good shape but the girl really got rawhided between the logs. She was in shock and her face so muddied she could hardly see. By the time we led them to a dry open place, helicopters were flying overhead. We waved but they kept going by and we got pretty desperate. Finally, one set down and carried the girl out to the hospital at Longview, then came back and picked up Reitan."

With these few words, the two rescuers moved on, anxious to view the devastation caused by the mudslides which already had poured from the Toutle River across Interstate Highway 5, blocking the main thoroughfare between Seattle and Portland, and then roared on into the Cowlitz River, where it overwhelmed homes, sawmills, boat marinas, and ships.

A different view of the eruption was viewed by a party of ten climbing Mount Adams. Fourteen-year-old David Larson was present and also John Christiansen and Fred Grimm, Seattle engineers. The climbers were only 500 feet from the summit when suddenly they watched the solid north face of St. Helens turn mushy and collapse. A second later there was a gigantic explosion which pulsed once, twice, and a third time, and then an enormous cloud rose miles into the air. Lightning crackled throughout it, creating so much static electricity that the climbers' ice picks buzzed and gave off sparks.

Fred Grimm declared, "It was windy on Mount Adams, but the wind stopped the moment of the eruption, as if sucked up in the blast, and didn't start up again for at least five minutes. We felt intense heat, and we were thirty-five miles away! A huge black cloud blotted out the sunlight and then started spewing ash. At first we were pelted with fine fragments, then pebbles, then larger pieces and singed pine cones. We forgot about climbing because the show went on so long it was time to get down off Mount Adams."

What about Harry Truman? According to a reporter who visited him the day before, the old man was as talkative as ever, stopping only to show off some of the hundreds of letters received from fans who had seen him on television. He was especially proud of one from Washington's much-publicized woman governor, Dixy Lee Ray. She wrote, "Your independence and straightforwardness is a fine example for all of us, particularly for senior citizens. When everyone else involved in the Mount St. Helens' eruption [March 27] appeared to be overcome by all the excitement, you stuck to what you knew and what common sense and experience told you."

Friends claimed Harry waved that letter around like it was a flag, chortling, "Hey, that lady needs me on her staff!"

No matter how much common sense, or stubbornness, he possessed, it didn't help him that violent Sunday morning. About five minutes after the eruption, Harry, his pets, his antiques which included a pink-and-gold 1957 Cadillac once owned by Elvis Presley, his neighbors in the A-frame, even a big segment of the lake he loved so dearly were buried under sixty feet of superheated muck and steaming logs. Later, when his sister and a long-time neighbor who had evacuated, heard the tragic news, both declared, "Harry always said he'd never be buried in a cemetery. He wanted to be buried near the lake. Well, he got his wish."

No one likes to talk about how many loggers would have died had the eruption occurred on a work day. Ordinarily more than two hundred, the majority employed by Weyerhaeuser Lumber Company, are at work on the north slope. Some drive to and from the logging areas in their own pickups or on motorcycles. Others stay in bunkhouses or with their families in trailers. On Sundays the work shuts down, the men go fishing or drive to small town markets or the larger communities such as Vancouver and Longview. When the volcano blew that Sunday morning, logger George Fickett was at his home near the north fork of the Toutle River. "I heard the goldangdest noise in Kingdom Come, like a bunch of upended oil drums banging down the road. Next there was a roar worse than a jet plane, and a lot of popping and snapping noises. Well, I know the sounds trees make when they're fallin', so I piled in the car and drove off down the road, only two shakes ahead of calamity. Good thing I did. There's nothing left up there now."

Danny Balch and Brian Thomas, employees of the Longview Fiber Plant, had pitched a tent along the Green River, as did friends Bruce Nelson and Sue Ruff, and Terry Crall and Karen Varner. All looked forward to a weekend of fishing and volcano watching. The earthquakes Sunday morning jarred them awake. Thomas peered through the tent opening just as a fearful roar pained his ears. Seconds later the campsite was bombarded with falling trees and limbs and a fiery cloud, orange and red and streaked with lightning, soared from the summit. Screaming at his companions to race for their cars, he crawled from his tent, only to be hurtled by the shock wave under a falling tree. Within five seconds a rain of burning ash and debris turned morning light into darkness, roared past, knocking over more trees and tearing shrubs out of the forest duff. Balch remembers the noise and swift darkness, trailing Thomas outside and groping about while calling his friends. He clutched at logs, unaware they were scorching hot, and severely burned his hands and bare feet. In spite of excruciating pain, he kept shouting for Thomas. Later—how much later neither knew—he felt something clutch one leg. When he reached down to free himself, he felt a human hand. It was Thomas, half-buried under a log that had crushed his right hip. After the noise of the holocaust abated, he and Thomas yelled for their friends. There was no answer from Crall and Varner, buried under steaming debris, but Nelson and Ruff pawed their way free, their mouths filled with mud, gagging as they inhaled the acrid gas. They spat out the mud, pulled their sweatshirts up over their noses, and tried to help free Thomas. None could budge the tree pinning him to the ground. When the light improved the three told him, "We're going for help."

"Don't leave me," Thomas begged.

Although Balch's arms and shoulders were so burned the skin hung in shreds, he shouted at Thomas, "We've got to get help. Don't move! Don't give up!"

The three set out, Nelson and Ruff guiding the still bare-footed Balch, now almost delirious with pain. The ground was covered with smoking ash. Every stump and rock radiated heat. After stumbling four miles, Balch collapsed. Feeling around until they found a patch where the ash had cooled, they laid Balch down and pressed on. By later afternoon they plodded into an open area and, spying helicopters cruising overhead, stripped off their sweat shirts and waved them until one of the rescue craft landed. The pilot radioed the information they gave him about the approximate position and injuries of their two surviving companions and the buried couple. When word was relayed back that rescuers would zero in on Balch and Thomas, the helicopter sped Bruce Nelson and Sue Ruff to a hospital. The next morning they learned that the two injured companions had been located and brought out to another hospital. For them, the long hideous ordeal was over.

Not all logging closed down that fateful morning. Of four men thinning trees twelve miles northwest of the summit, only one is alive today. According to James Scymanky, thirty-six, of Woodburn, Oregon, he and Leonty Skorohodoff, thirty, and Evlanty Sharipoff, forty, of Mount St. Angel were working while a fourth, Jose Dias, thirty-three, a Mexican-American from Stockton, California, walked up the steep slope to their pickup for a needed tool. "All of a sudden," Scymanky would tell reporters later, "Dias came running toward us, hollering, 'The volcano blew up!' Next we heard this horrible hissing sound, a frying blast hit us, and we were in darkness. We yelled to each other that boiling lava probably was rolling down on us and we better run. Only we couldn't. I guess there wasn't enough oxygen in the hot air because every time we took a breath, we coughed and choked something awful. You know how it is when you've dove into a pool and run out of air before you get to the surface? That's the way our lungs felt.

"Suddenly I got knocked over and my hard hat fell off. I slammed it back on and the four of us crawled over the trees we had cut. We'd stacked them good, but now they were scattered all over by the blast, I guess. Even though we always wear heavy gloves when working, the wood was so hot it burned through to our hands. We headed downhill where we knew there was a small spring. The water was muddy and warm now, but we fell into it, rolling over and over and splashing water on our faces and heads because everyone of us had burns everywhere, and the pain was terrible. Maybe an hour later when the hissing let up and there was a little more light, we decided to climb to the pickup and if the motor hadn't been damaged, try to drive out to a hospital. I'm telling you, we all were in agony. Anyway, we made it to the truck, only it was busted up. The climbing and breathing hot ash and so much pain had worn us to a frazzle. We rested maybe an hour until the light improved and then started walking. The road was littered with fallen trees that looked like they'd been run through a peeler. Every step we stirred more hot dust. Putting handkerchiefs over our noses didn't help much.

"Don't ask me how long it took, but we came to this place where the debris and ash was stacked over a hundred feet high. Sharipoff straggled off to find a way around it. Skorohodoff and I tried to stop him, but didn't have the strength. He wandered out of sight and we never saw him again. The three of us finally sat down in a place where maybe rescue planes could see us. I guess the only thing that kept us sane was the thought that somebody would get us out of that hellhole. Nine hours later it happened. Two fellows in a 'copter risked their necks setting that bird down, picked us up and flew us to a Portland hospital's burn treatment center. It was too late for Dias and Skorohodoff, who died the next day."

In spite of having second- and third-degree burns over 50 percent of his body, Scymanky survived, but faced months of hospitalization. Eventually Sharipoff's body was found. The news made Scymanky wonder aloud, "All those hours on the mountain, we knew we were dying. Now I'm wondering why I was the only one to survive, only I guess I'll never know the answer."

Stories of those who witnessed and survived the devastating aftermath of the eruption would fill another hundred pages, or more. The tally of those dead and missing fluctuated for days. The official search ended Sunday, June 1, with the casualty count totaling 22 known dead and 55 missing. Admittedly, those figures would change as more remains were recovered. Although the organized air search by the Army and the Washington National Guard helicopters ended then, the responsibility for further search and rescue was turned over to local county sheriffs and their deputies. A few individuals would not give up searching for lost relatives and continued their sorry task for weeks, without success.

There is one more story chosen as the concluding one for this chapter. It involves an eight-pound mutt of poodle-terrier mix found in a totally devastated area. Perhaps because she was so small she found refuge in a moist dark hollow amidst the falling trees and searing heat. After the roaring abated and the air was still, the tiny creature began scratching for air. When she cleared a passage to the surface, she found herself trapped. Days later members of a search-and-rescue team, airlifted onto the mountain, discovered the bodies of a young man and woman, their arms around each other, crushed between falling trees. While the rescuers exhumed the bodies, they were astounded to hear small whimpering sounds.

One of the men whistled softly. The answer was a weak but joyful yelp.

Digging like badgers, the men soon lifted a dirty, emaciated, black-and-white female dog from her prison and gave her water. The man who cuddled her in his arms had tears in his eyes. "It's a miracle, a bloomin' miracle! But we gotta get her to a vet. She's gonna have pups."

Within an hour the waif was handed over to the staff at the Cowlitz County animal shelter in Longview. They provided a dry warm cage, water, special food, and tender loving care. After a discussion she was given a new name, Poodley-Mama, since she was part poodle, part terrier. The next day she posed beautifully for press and television photographers. When the photos appeared nationwide, animal lovers inundated the shelter with offers for new homes.

On June 2, Poodley-Mama delivered three healthy pups, two black and one white. But complications developed and a veterinarian had to perform a Caesarian operation to remove a fourth still-born puppy. By this time Poodley-Mama was running a very high fever, and the staff feared she might not survive. Between the medication and intravenous feedings, she did pull through. Seven weeks later the healthy mama and her thriving offspring were handed over to new, carefully chosen families.

4.

An Overview of Destruction

a hundred more tales could describe the plight of victims of the eruption and still not provide an overview of the destruction. Fortunately, there are thousands of photographs taken by a special unit of the Oregon Air National Guard which portray the damage from the crater, down the forks of the Toutle River, along the Cowlitz and the Columbia rivers, and the ashfall 500 miles eastward into Montana. Since the aircraft employed is a Grumman OVI Mohawk, the same type of plane used for aerial enemy surveillance in Vietnam, the project is called Mohawk Unit, 1042nd Military Intelligence, U.S. Army. There are only five such Units throughout the world: one based in Oregon, two in Georgia, one each in Germany and Korea. Training exercises for the Oregon Unit include assisting the U.S. Forest Service, U.S. Fish and Wildlife Service, and the U.S. Coast and Geodetic Survey. The twin-engine turboprop Mohawk resembles a bulky military transport, yet carries only a pilot and co-pilot who serves as a combination navigator and surveillance systems operator. The systems include cameras installed in the belly, nose cone, and sides, an infrared heat detector, and other instruments.

According to Sergeant Douglas Fogg of Ashland, the Mohawk Unit photographed wisps of steam rising from two small holes on the normally solid icy summit *eighteen months* before the first mild tremor beneath the volcano was recorded. Sergeant Fogg explained, "Usually we flew over the summit about once a month while spotting fires for the Forest Service. As the holes grew larger, we used the infrared heat detector to monitor the heat being released by the supposedly dormant volcano. After the first earthquake on March 20 was followed by many small ones, we monitored the area four times weekly. As the situation intensified, we flew as much as three to four-times daily."

On Sunday, May 18, Sergeant Fogg participated in a weekend Oregon National Guard drill near Salem. "During the morning briefing session, about 9:30 A.M., word reached us that Mount St. Helens had blown its top. The commander assigned one air crew to photograph the volcano and the North and South Forks of the Toutle. Warrant Officer Andy Rux piloted the Mohawk and I served as systems operator.

"As we framed the area in our flight paths, I kept a running observation record and also took exposures with a hand-held camera. We flew at elevations ranging from 2,000 to 14,000 feet, photographing the plume, the new crater, the flattened timber, the mudslides advancing down the Toutle into the

Cowlitz and the Columbia, and the first search-and-rescue planes and helicopters on the scene. It was awesome."

This was the first time in history that a lengthy and minutely detailed photographic reconnaissance of an *active* volcano was carried out. For decades to come the information would provide scientists with invaluable evidence on which to base further studies.

Although many young readers and their parents are somewhat familiar with stories of the violent eruptions of Mount Vesuvius, Krakatoa, and other volcanoes, those happened so long ago and so far away that probably few among the throngs of sightseers and television viewers watching Mount St. Helens perform gave much thought to the aftermath. They hoped to see mushroom-shaped clouds, a superproduction of fireworks, maybe even burning lava overtaking the upper slopes. Most just took for granted that everything the volcano spouted would go straight up, and come right down again. Then the big show would be over, like the fireworks displays at Fourth of July celebrations.

Unfortunately, Mount St. Helens' major eruption was far more lethal and widespread than anticipated. Thus, a brief overview of the far-reaching havoc is included now. Following chapters will describe in greater detail the destruction of Spirit Lake, the loss of millions of board feet of timber and logging equipment, the heroic efforts of search-and-rescue teams, the cleanup, the ashfall, wildlife ravaged, the spoilation of an important estuary, and the threat to ocean-going freighters plying the Columbia from Vancouver downstream to the Pacific Ocean.

When Mount St. Helens blew its top, the big bang was heard 200 miles in every direction. This active volcano may yet produce more eruptions and quiver and steam for a quarter century, so the present elevation of 8,364 feet may change again and again. It could be shorn to its very roots or, amazingly, it could rebuild its cone foot by foot over several hundred or thousand years until it equals or has surpassed its pre-eruption summit.

Scientists calculate that the May 18 blast equaled the force of a hydrogen bomb, or 500 times greater than the atomic bomb dropped on Hiroshima, ejecting an estimated cubic mile of earth skyward. The former craters are now one, a cavity one mile wide, almost two miles long, and 2,100 feet deep. The crater is never quiet because of a constant hissing, puffing, and steaming and countless small avalanches. However, previous studies revealed an eruption equal to that occurred nearly 2,000 years before Christ was born, and again at approximately 100-year periods, with large lava flows pouring out in A.D. 100, 200, and 300. A thousand-year sleep began then, but was broken briefly around A.D. 850 and again in 1400. Still more lava and pyroclastic flows filled the throat and surfaced in the fourteenth, fifteenth, and mid-seventeenth centuries. A few white fur traders and pioneers left descriptions in their journals, and famed Canadian artist, Paul Kane, sketched an eruption on March 26, 1847, one of a chain which began in 1842 and continued into 1857. Once again the volcano quieted until its 1980 outbreak.

The nature of volcanoes being what it is, the cycles of quiet and violence will continue. In fact, Mount St. Helens has already begun its rebuilding process. Aerial surveys and penetration of the new crater during quiet periods by teams of scientists have revealed that a dome or plug of lava is moving upward from the throat. Within a month after the

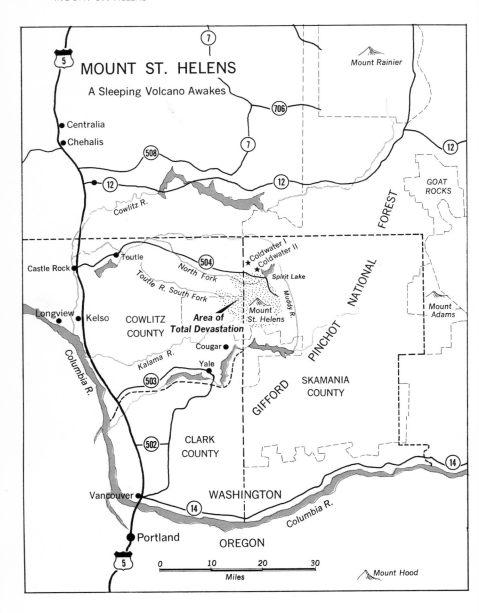

eruption the dome measured 660 feet in width and 200 feet in height, and was rising about 20 feet daily. This dome could be destroyed in future eruptions but eventually a new and stable cone will take shape. If and when that happens, it could be because, miles below, pressure is being released through other vents and St. Helens' neighboring peaks will stage noisy extravaganzas for generations to come.

At 8:32 A.M. on that never-to-be-forgotten Sunday and a few seconds later:

• The swollen north face of Mount St. Helens collapsed.

• A plume of steam jetted skyward, turning black as it soared, roared, and created its own lightning.

• Searing gas, chunks of rock, and melting ice shot out the *side* of the weakened notched north slope in a wholly unanticipated way known to have occurred only once before in eons of volcanic eruptions.

• The blast spread fanwise at speeds from 100 to 150 miles per hour, mowing down everything in its path, even shearing stout evergreens of their bark and limbs.

• A cubic mile of pulverized rock, illuminated with purple lightning, soared 14 miles in the sky while producing unearthly fireworks whick kept viewers mesmerized for hours.

• An avalanche of mud and melted snow and ice overwhelmed the South Fork of the Toutle for 25 miles, burying homes, ranches, livestock, bridges and roads, and the lower stretch of the town of Toutle.

• The water level in the Swift Creek reservoir, the uppermost of three strung along the Lewis River south of

59

the volcano, rose 13 feet within minutes, but thanks to the precautions taken by the utility company it did not overrun its banks nor burst the sturdy dam downstream.

• Another avalanche downed timber on the north slope and bombarded Spirit Lake, sending millions of gallons of water across the lake and then plugging the outlet with a dam of mud and debris which, by nightfall, was 200 feet high.

• The lake water and avalanche inundated the valley downstream 20 miles west of the lake.

• On top of this incalculable destruction a pyroclastic flow of boiling ash and water gushed from the throat, or vent, and at speeds up to 200 miles per hour dropped tons more of scalding mud and debris which overran the forks of the Toutle, destroyed giant-sized logging machinery, locomotives, railroad cars and trucks stacked with logs, and knocked out a railroad bridge on its great rampage.

• Alerted that the mudflow soon would overtake the Interstate 5 highway bridge spanning the Toutle, highway patrolmen raced to place barriers across it only moments before the boiling waters poured over and under the bridge.

• The swelling mudflow carrying logs, steel girders, battered houses, vehicles, and dead animals overwhelmed the Cowlitz, raising its channel by 15 feet and tossing marina docks, boats, and even freighters like twigs.

• Still unchecked, the flood muddied the estuary at the mouth of the Cowlitz, then silted up the normal 40-

foot-deep Columbia shipping channel with 14 feet of muck and imperiled shipping traffic with waves and churning rafts of logs.

There was still more havoc wrought by ash. Eleven miles overhead ash clouds tumbled and boiled and then, pushed by strong west winds, sped eastward across Washington, turning daylight into darkness and dumping up to seven inches of the pyroclastic particles on towns, crops, and orchards. Traffic stalled, schools and airports closed, cars and trucks skidded off roads, people inhaled the stinking dust, their eyes smarting and lungs burning. By midafternoon of this "Ash Sunday," Spokane, Washington, was in darkness and almost paralyzed by the ashfall, then northern Idaho, and on Monday morning highways, airports, schools, and even rail operations from Missoula, Montana, to Williston, North Dakota, were shut down. Kentucky and Tennessee reported a light dusting by midday and northern Virginia by evening.

Now a monumental task faced thousands of Americans: search and rescue, digging out, cleaning up, figuring losses in the billions of property, timber, wildlife, fish and birds, all the while wondering when Mount St. Helens might erupt again.

5.

Search and Rescue

he first planes and helicopters airborne transported those who knew the area well —the once-snowy heights, the lower slopes crosshatched with timber, blue lakes, sparkling streams, and flower-strewn meadows. Geologists, foresters, sheriffs' deputies, news photographers, Air National Guard personnel—they lifted off airstrips at Portland, Vancouver, Longview, and Seattle, the countryside green below but the sky dominated by that awesome stinking, roaring, black column of steam and ash shot through with lightning. Flying was hazardous because of the turbulence wrought by the eruption. The shock waves and lateral blasts had petered out but visibility was marred by steam and smoke rising from smouldering fires, falling ash, and debris. Chattering teletypes

and radio receivers and jangling telephones h
the pilots and passengers what to expect. Not
tightened their seat belts and readied their can
recorders, they were looking down, horror-stric
ished land smothered in death-gray ash.

Some burst into tears. A few swore to ease their shock.
"Hey, where's Spirit Lake? It should be right over . . . it's
gone! And look at those mudflows and log jams on the Toutle!
And the trees! The whole forest has been knocked flat!"

A pilot points to an object below, and circles. It is a pickup
truck, the frame caved in and buried to its windows in ash.
The camerman switches to binoculars and winces, then fo-
cuses his lens on two twisted bodies on the roof of the cab.
He films the scene.

The plane carrying a news team of *The Columbian* had a
dual priority: take photographs and, God willing, find their
co-worker, Reid Blackburn, who had manned remote-control
cameras from observation post Coldwater I. He'd been all
but glued to the slopes the past three weeks and yesterday
had refused an invitation to drive to Olympia for a seafood
dinner with Fay, his bride, and friends. So he was alone up
there, sitting in his Volvo that morning, and died instantly,
suffocated by the intense heat and the ash that buried his
car to the rooftop. The car was spotted quickly and circled
from above while friends anxiously scanned the ash for footprints. There were none.

Three times that afternoon Dwight Reber of Columbia Helicopters risked his life in vain efforts to land near the Volvo.
"The trees were lying flat in a west-northwest direction, many
smouldering and burning. From an altitude of 100 feet you
could feel intense heat from the ground. Nearby I could see

.tretches of the Toutle where the water was actually boiling, and a Weyerhaeuser log-sorting yard where huge trucks were twisted like pretzels and logs scattered every which way. I didn't dare land. On the last trip clouds moved in and visibility was so poor I had to pull out."

Nearly a week passed before conditions improved enough so that Blackburn's body could be removed.

Another plane under contract to the Forest Service was also buzzing the slope, its passengers searching for any trace of Dr. David Johnston and the Coldwater II post trailer. Not only the site but the entire area was buried in steaming ash. These men knew about Dr. Johnston's excited last words, "Vancouver! Vancouver! This is it!" They also knew that somehow, perhaps due to faulty transmission, the message was never recorded at the Vancouver headquarters. Instead, a ham radio operator picked it up, relayed it immediately to the dispatch center, and tried repeatedly to establish contact with Dr. Johnston.

Later, at a news briefing, geologists would explain that both observation posts were directly in the path of the completely unexpected lateral or horizontal blast of superheated gas and debris, and the concussion pulverized everything in its range. One geologist described it as "a planetary cannon blast."

Still, courageous pilots and searchers lifted 150 victims off the lower slopes that Sunday, and also those stranded by the Toutle's flooding and log jams which had torn out sections of roads and bridges. Scores were taken to evacuation centers or, if need be, to hospitals. Among these were the injured survivors described in Chapter 3.

In mountain country heavily used by hunters, fishermen, skiers, campers, and hikers, accidents are rather frequent. Years before, county law enforcement agencies, fire department and local volunteer emergency squads underwent rigorous first aid and search-and-rescue schooling. Area by area, routines were drawn up to deal with small catastrophes. However, those first few flights revealed the enormity of the disaster. Obviously a great deal more assistance was needed, so requests were made to state and federal agencies. Troops, aircraft, and equipment were ordered out from the U.S. Army base at Fort Lewis, near Seattle. Twenty-five helicopters zeroed in on the single runway airport at Toledo in Lewis County, west of the volcano and on the banks of the Cowlitz River about eight miles north of its confluence with the Toutle. By nightfall the airport reminded veterans of small military bases in Vietnam. The next day craft from National Guard companies of Washington, Oregon, and Wyoming joined the rescue force. A tent morgue was raised, but cordoned off from curious sightseers and the press. When newsmen protested vigorously, one corpsman quipped, "We got enough to do without trippin' over you guys. Give our regrets to Walter [Cronkite]."

Lewis County Sheriff William Wiester reported one volunteer crew walked in mud up to the armpits while looking for bodies along riverbanks. Also, he added, donations of food and money were pouring in, and being used to supply emergency shelters. A dozen women worked around the clock preparing meals and survival kits for search crews. The same, Wiester stressed, was going on in Skamania and Cowlitz counties. Hundreds of citizens volunteered labor and equipment to assist the county emergency search-and-rescue units. One rescuer informed reporters, "Day One and Two we brought the living off the mountain. From Day Three on, we sought the dead and missing."

National Guardsmen are familiar with the heartbreaking aftermath of hurricanes, tornadoes, fires, floods, and even riots, but Mount St. Helens had left a serious block to rescue efforts: the ash on the north slope was still so hot in places that it burned off the soles of combat boots, and many mounds proved too unstable to support 'copters, four-wheel drive vehicles, and, in some instances, searchers.

After the ash cooled, an effective aid was the search dog. Several were employed to good advantage. One named Hauser was a 100-pound German shepherd, two-and-a-half-years old and trained by Lewis County Deputy Sheriff Brian Hill. Both were members of a twelve man-three dog S&R (search-and-rescue) team based at Salkum. For days after the eruption helicopters sought Meta Lake, now buried under volcanic ash, and between three and five persons known to have been camping there. Finally a 'copter hovering only a few feet above ground scattered the ash covering two bodies, but could not land. A half dozen searchers accompanied by Deputy Hill and his dog hiked in from a staging area where helicopters could set down. Hauser was turned loose and began sniffing and circling after the two bodies were bagged. A search dog can detect a human scent under thirty feet of powder snow, yet in cooled ash, now dubbed "Cascade cement," it cannot locate victims buried more than three feet. Soon Hauser paused, sniffed and pawed, sniffed more, and started digging. The first object uncovered was a beer can. With his handler on his knees, urging, "Find 'em, boy, find 'em!" the dog exposed a patch of dark substance. The handler then explored the find cautiously and informed his companions, "It feels like bones and flesh." The dog was withdrawn, barking excitedly, and small wonder. The men dug out the remains of a cooked chicken! But still deeper there was a sleeping bag, a small tent, and inside it—nothing. Again Hauser was turned loose and after a discouraging search found the remains of a man and a woman. These were also bagged and carried to the helicopter, while Hauser continued working until the missing third man was located.

Another morning Hill and Hauser joined a search party of four helicopters and reserves of the U.S. Army Third Squadron, Air Fifth Cavalry Regiment. The object was to locate the bodies of two loggers known to have been bucking logs near Elk Lake, nine miles northwest of Mount St. Helens. Three craft descended gingerly onto the unstable ground while the fourth circled overhead, maintaining radio contact with a volcano-watch communications plane patrolling at a higher elevation. As soon as the dust settled, the searchers and Hauser checked the area, uncovering partially buried logs, uprooted trees, and the remains of a water tank and pickup. Hill explained later, "There was little talk. We were all aware of our dangerous position, but you can't think about that. You have a job to do, and get on with it even when the ground shakes so at times you can hardly keep your balance. We kept one ear cocked for any warning from the 'copter overhead that bad weather was moving in fast, as it does often in the Cascades. There are always alternate plans so we can leave quickly and regroup at some safer location.

"You ask if Hauser found the bodies? Yes, but they were so wedged in a log jam we couldn't remove them until another party came in with tools and sawed out sections of timber so they could be freed." Deputy Hill concluded his story by saying, "Hauser and I will keep looking for bodies as long as our bosses let us."

A Seattle photographer was able to photograph the eruption, his flight, and rescue, and even record his thoughts on his tape recorder. Dave Crockett, twenty-eight, was standing on a logging road a mile west of Mount St. Helens when it blew. As the black plume formed, he jumped into his car and raced for safety, dropping down into a gully. Before he reached it the small bridge at the bottom, which spanned a stream, burst as it was hit with a torrent of mud and debris. Quickly putting the gear in reverse, Crockett glanced back, only to see the forest on the heights being flattened. He was trapped between the two. He shouted into his recorder, "The road exploded in front of me . . . it's hard to breathe . . . my eyes are full of ash."

Grabbing his equipment, he left the car and raced up the near ridge which served as a wall between him and the blast. Since it had been clear-cut of timber, he was not threatened with falling timber but a blizzard of ash turned day into night. "Right now I think I'm dead," he recorded, coughing and fighting for his breath. It was then he realized that the deadly blast had gone over him, leaving him uninjured. He dropped to his knees and thanked God for his miraculous escape.

Suddenly he jumped up, shook his fist at the roaring mountain, and yelled, "You didn't get me!" and then busied himself with his camera. Knowing it would be some time before aircraft ventured into the area, he gathered wood for three signal fires. It was midafternoon before he saw helicopters, and lighted his fires. As one craft hovered, and descended slowly to rescue him, he filmed that, and the liftoff. The film and tape cassette made a whopping good story.

Not all the attention was focused on the volcano slopes. Fifteen helicopters of the Washington National Guard and as many more from the Air Force Reserve, State Patrol, and

Oregon National Guard airlifted an estimated 2,000 persons from flooded areas or sites stranded when mudflows or log jams wiped out roads and bridges, principally along the Toutle, Kalama, Muddy, and Lewis rivers. Most landed at Longview or Kelso airports where they were able to contact relatives or friends for shelter, or were moved to emergency shelters such as the Cascade Middle School in Longview.

Meanwhile, a stream of four-legged refugees were airlifted or driven to the Cowlitz County Humane Society shelter in Longview. Within twenty-four hours its pens and cages were crowded and an adjacent field filled with cattle, horses, goats, and chickens. Twelve volunteers answered calls to haul animals swept into the rivers and now floundering on mudflats. Many died from shock or their frantic efforts to pull themselves out of the mud. The Center also accepted pets of families housed in evacuation shelters. As the Society's supplies of feed were exhausted quickly, a radio appeal resulted in over two tons of pet food and livestock feed being donated by the Purina pet food company.

Near Castle Rock cattle and horses on the bottomland ranches along the lower Toutle and Cowlitz rivers were caught in the mudflows. Some drowned, some were injured by tossing logs and died, some were mired in muck, unable to move, only their heads exposed. By the time ranchers and volunteers assembled at various locations, the mud was hardening to almost concretelike consistency, yet was extremely slippery. One rancher inflated two tire tubes, fashioned slings for his feet and, carrying rope and a shovel, "skated" out to help his beleaguered stock. Others laid sections of corrugated roofing and siding on the ground to form a stable path for men and animals. Another attached a hastily rigged sled to a tractor winch, drove out as far as he could, wound rope harnesses around the victims and gently skidded them to firm ground. Helicopter pilot Larry Quick employed a stout net to lift twenty-seven head of cattle out of the muck, and the grateful rancher presented him a fine milk cow as payment.

By late Tuesday the Red Cross disaster-inquiry office at Longview had received 3,700 calls since 9:00 A.M. Sunday. Here are a few reports from that source.

An overnight backpack trip to entertain their daughter Bonnie Lu, four, turned into a nightmare for Mike and Lu Moore of Castle Rock. They could not have chosen a safer location, they thought, when they parked their car twelve miles and two high ridges north of Mount St. Helens on Saturday, May 17. The parents packed their lightweight tent, gear, and food up a gently sloping forest trail, Lu carrying three-month-old Terra in the lead, then Bonnie Lu, and lastly Mike. The weather was beautiful and that night the family slept well. On Sunday morning Lu was preparing breakfast when she heard a rumbling noise and felt the ground shake. Hurriedly she and Mike loaded their backpacks, Mike carried Bonnie Lu and Lu the baby, and all hurried toward a small trail shelter used by hunters. By the time they reached it an enormous black cloud thundered overhead and lightning struck in every direction. Quickly they wrapped socks over the girls' mouths and noses, and their own, and huddled closely, the parents' bodies protecting their children.

They were in total darkness for an hour, maybe two. When daylight returned they stepped out into a different scene. Fallen branches and trees and a heavy coating of ash blocked the trail and made the pathway almost unrecognizable. Fortunately, Mike, an experienced outdoorsman, got his bearings and was able to lead his family over obstacles toward their car. They never reached it because the way was entirely blocked by debris. Sensibly, Mike set up the tent and Lu resumed preparing a meal, all the while reassuring Bonnie Lu and explaining that they would spend another night in the tent. Maybe, tomorrow, there would be a b-i-g surprise.

Monday afternoon a rescue helicopter responded to Mike's signals and tried to land, but raised too much dust. Next, the pilot hovered while crewmen let down a rope ladder and safety net. One man inched his way down and assisted the parents, each with a child, in attaining the 'copter and then climbed to his seat, pulling in the harness and closing the door. The Moores were transported to a hospital, examined for injuries and after-effects of ash inhalation, and then released, smiling, to relatives who drove them home.

Another family was not as fortunate. Ron and Barbara Siebold of Olympia spent many weekends camping on Mount St. Helens with their daughter Michele, nine, and son Kevin, seven. They knew the location of improved Forest Service campgrounds and more secluded clearings near logging roads where all could watch wildlife and Ron could photograph deer, goats, flowers, and birds. A neighbor said of them, "That mountain was their home away from home. They were always camping together."

About 8:30 Sunday morning they were easing up Highway 504 in the family's Chevy Blazer, windows down to enjoy the clean air and birdsong. Ron figured they were at least ten miles on the west or "safe" side of the first roadblock. Yet seconds later all four died, suffocated by the searing blast. Their bodies were among the first removed, along with the remains of a Hawthorne, California, couple, Fred and Margery

Rollins, found totally dehydrated beside their car.

Whenever 'copters landed near abandoned vehicles which were checked out, orange spray paint was used to mark X or OK on them to inform other searchers that the area or object had been investigated. Thus, two days after the eruption, a Huey helicopter from the 54th Medical Detachment of the 9th Infantry Division, Fort Lewis, passed over a battered Chevrolet pickup from which the bodies of two men and two boys had been removed, and the truck roof marked. The Huey set down on an open section of a former logging road where several large cranes and four huge logging trucks were lying askew, partly buried in ash. The site had to be checked again because relatives had informed the Red Cross that Paul Schmidt of Silverton, Oregon, an amateur photographer, was still missing. Since he drove a red Toyota sedan, license number CTR 460, it didn't take long to locate a fragment of bright red metal against the gray ash. Crewmen walked toward it gingerly, their boots sinking into the ash that was cool on top but more than 200 degrees Fahrenheit two feet below. With brooms and shovels they uncovered enough to see a briefcase and sleeping bag inside the car, but no body. One crewman examined the briefcase and found a wallet and credit cards which confirmed that the Toyota was that of Paul Schmidt. The remaining corpsmen walked a mile along the blast-scoured road without finding any trace of the man. All they could guess was that Schmidt had parked his car, shouldered his cameras, and hiked up the road to the point where it crested a ridge, in order to have an unobstructed view of the volcano. The searchers returned to the Toyota, sprayed on the orange X, gathered up Schmidt's possessions, and within an hour delivered them to authorities at the Toledo airstrip. They, in turn, forwarded them to the family.

One of the most dramatic aerial photographs, viewed nationwide, revealed the bare body of an unidentified young boy sprawled in the back of a pickup truck, his clothes peeled off by the blast. A helicopter assigned to the 304th Air Force Reserve Squadron landed close by. Since the license plate number matched that provided by relatives, the crew identified the victims as Day Karr of Renton and son Andy, eleven inside the cab and son Mike, nine, in the back. The vehicle was parked at the end of a logging road close by the South Fork of the Toutle River, only three miles from the mountain.

The news media devoted much space to crediting pilots and crews who fought adverse flying conditions and countless dangers in their search-and-rescue efforts. None could be faulted. Nevertheless, a number of complaints were registered. Some were the expected petty frettings of individuals who didn't like the food served at evacuation centers, or the cots, or crying children. Others, distraught with worry about missing relatives known to have ventured onto the mountain, wandered from one information center to the other, to sheriffs' offices, newspapers, and shelters, trying to glean scraps of information. The lists of dead and missing could not help but vary from day to day, causing many to be upset and rail about "bureaucratic bungling."

Some complaints about poor coordination were justified. During the first three days of search and rescue, the sheriffs of Skamania, Lewis, and Cowlitz counties communicated with their field men, each employing a separate radio frequency. Due to the overwhelming amount of information crisscrossing between headquarters and search parties, there was little time to pool or exchange information. Worse, there was no overall coordinator of search-and-rescue efforts. Each hard-working squad did its best.

Relatives and reporters traveled unnecessary distances when air search centers shifted from Toutle to Kelso to Toledo and Salkum without advance notice or reasons given. The press complained that no one person seemed in charge. Local and state agencies had had nearly two months for planning, yet the state had not come up with a single coordinated search-and-information center. Personnel at rescue staging areas could not communicate with one another because of incompatible radio frequencies. Press access was hampered by barriers. Relatives of some missing persons were furious when not permitted on search flights. The bald fact was that the flights were dangerous and there was room aboard only for trained personnel.

By this time hundreds more state and federal employees had been dispatched to the area. They were assigned to the state Department of Emergency Services, Washington State Patrol, Federal Emergency Management Agency, U. S. Army and Air Force Reserves, Forest Service, Geological Survey, U. S. Army, National Guard, Federal Bureau of Investigation, Center for Disease Control, and others where victims could apply for welfare assistance, flood and disaster insurance claims, loans for rebuilding, food stamps, emergency fuel rations, clothing, household supplies, and child care.

Actually, someone was very much in charge of National Guard tactical operations. For two months preceding May 18, squadrons flew reconnaissance missions throughout the area, devising plans should the Guard be summoned to mount an operation there. The decision to use the Toledo airport was sound. It was a World War II auxiliary field with an excellent runway. On May 17 helicopters flew a practice mission to Yakima, and the crews set up camp. Early Sunday morning fuel trucks rolled in, but refueling was interrupted by the eruption, which disabled a third of the aircraft and the fuel carriers. The remaining 'copters lifted off and flew to Fort Lewis for instructions. When flying conditions permitted, they returned to the Kelso airport and operated from there for three days when the Toledo runway was once more in operation.

One pilot who flew long hours of search and rescue those first three days resented the rumor that nobody was in charge. "We were running the show. We had it wired. We had a high bird and a low bird. Ours was a concentrated search-and-rescue effort. We rescued more than 130 people that first day [May 18], 15 the second day, 1 the third. We didn't miss any survivors nor lose a single bird or man in spite of some foul weather."

According to a press report on May 21, Gene Smith, Forest Service fire manager, was named coordinator of all rescue operations. He and his staff compiled a master list of the dead and missing and circulated it to all units and the press, and another list of the names and locations of those in charge of operations in the several areas. County rescue units soon shared compatible radio frequencies. Pilots produced a master grid plan, with aircraft and ground parties assigned specific areas. There was almost no further duplication and shortly after fourteen bodies were recovered, and others later.

On Thursday, May 22, President Carter and his entourage appeared. Governor Ray, who was also running for reelection, had telephoned and dispatched a storm of appeals to federal agencies and to the President for disaster relief. She welcomed the opportunity to describe the situation face-to-face with the President.

Carter and his party saw the area from a helicopter which, at times, dipped within 200 feet of the ravaged earth. However, he never saw Mount St. Helens because the volcano was hidden in low-lying clouds. After the flight he was driven to Longview to visit a Red Cross emergency shelter, then to Kelso, threatened by a mudslide from Spirit Lake, and then to Forest Service headquarters in Vancouver to confer with federal, state, and local officials and the press. His first remarks were that the devastation was simply dreadful, but some day the volcano would rival the Grand Canyon as a tourist attraction. Perhaps Mount St. Helens should become part of a new national park. That way there would be an information and visitors center, ranger naturalists presenting lectures and films, guided nature walks, and marked trails similar to those in other National Parks.

Governor Ray immediately voiced opposition to the idea, even though the creation of a National Park would mean several million dollars being expended in the disaster area, employment to residents, and undoubtedly would draw thousands of visitors who would bolster the local economy. If there was going to be a new park there, she remarked, it would be a Washington *State* Park, not federally funded and controlled. If those in power instituted such a project, she, personally, would man barricades to keep out the feds.

Governor Ray seemed to have overlooked the fact that Mount St. Helens, Spirit Lake, and the devastated 150,000 acres had long been under federal control, being wholly within the boundaries of the Gifford Pinchot National Forest. For

At 3:30 P.M. clouds of ash were still pouring out of the volcano.

Mudflow in the South Fork of the Toutle River.

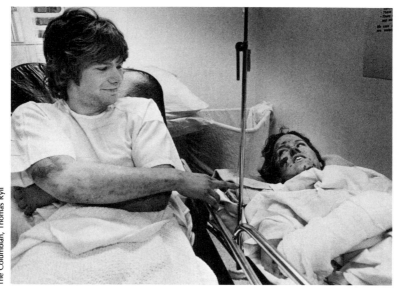

Venus Ann Dergan and Roald Reitan survived a terrifying journey in mud-and-log-filled Toutle River.

Search-and-rescue squad searches vehicle demolished during the eruption.

Ryan Lake campground with abandoned recreationist vehicles.

A National Guardsman searches tent for victims.

The Columbian, Jerry Coughlan

Muddy River log jam, southeast of Mount St. Helens.

USDA Forest Service, Jim Hughes

President Carter visiting the Gifford Pinchot National Forest volcano emergency communications center at Vancouver, Washington.

Looking south into Spirit Lake basin in June of 1980. The crater still steams in the background.

years there had been an information center, ranger programs, and marked nature trails at the lake for visitor use.

After Mr. Carter promised "every assistance within our means," the meeting adjourned. The President and his entourage flew back to the nation's capital, and Washingtonians resumed their search-and-rescue and cleanup labors.

The May 18 eruption caught the scientists off-guard. While seismographs correctly recorded the sharp 5.0 magnitude earthquake that Sunday morning, none gave any warning that a catastrophic eruption was imminent nor that the bulging north side would collapse outwardly. "Undoubtedly the quake triggered the eruption," one geologist remarked, "but until we change our recording and forecasting technologies, we can't anticipate so violent an eruption."

With the death of David Johnston weighing heavily on them, the Survey specialists renewed their studies. Before nightfall a few instruments were replaced on the volcano, and more in the ensuing weeks. There was no public mention of the risks the courageous Survey crews faced in carrying out their tasks. More remote-control cameras were also installed to photograph the peak in color every thirty seconds. Thus, the technician at the dispatch desk in Vancouver and the scientists there would observe the volcano closely on a television screen which reproduced the photographs. On cloudy days or during night hours when the peak was not visible, numbers flashing on computerized instruments and two seismographs kept them informed. In addition, information from the safety patrol plane was received there, and also transmitted to all working within the danger zone, including the crater, and to the standby helicopter charged with speedy removal of personnel whenever necessary.

Hampered frequently by intermittent cloud cover, winds, and rain, the official search terminated June 1 with 22 listed as missing. Helicopters returned to Fort Lewis. Army Reserve and Washington National Guard units, Lewis County Search and Rescue, Washington State Patrol, and all other squads withdrew, with the understanding they would be recalled should the volcano again wreak widespread damage. Until then it would be the responsibility of the individual sheriffs and their deputies to follow up any new search-and-rescue leads.

On that same date a Geological Survey press release stated that the volcano was in a quiet period and "seismic activity remains low." However, no one believed he or she had seen the end of Mount St. Helens' eruptions.

6.

Ash, Ash Everywhere

Tim and Susan Gilmore had left Yakima, 85 miles east of Mount St. Helens, that Sunday morning and were driving up a winding highway which would take them across 4,500-foot-high White Pass because its viewpoint parking area provided unobstructed views of snow-mantled Mount Rainier and Mount St. Helens. The car radio was on and suddenly the announcer interrupted his chatter with early reports of a major volcanic eruption.

Susan was excited. "We can see it from the top of the pass!"

Tim nodded and increased their speed. A few moments later when they were about five miles below the summit, they heard a light pattering noise on the car roof. Susan was disgusted. "Oh, just our luck! It's starting to rain!"

Tim squinted at the sky and saw a huge black cloud roiling overhead. He stretched an arm out the window. "It's not raining. That's ash falling!"

Almost instantly their visibility was reduced to a few yards and the hood and windshield of the car were plastered with ash. "The higher we climb, the more ash we'll get into. I'm heading back to Yakima," Tim decided. He switched on the headlights and windshield wipers, slowed and made a rapid U-turn. Within five minutes he was forced to reduce their speed to ten miles per hour and could barely see the taillights of a camper ahead of them. Lightning crackled too close for comfort and thunder rocked the car. The air smelled strongly like a burned-out building. The road was covered with an inch of fine dust stirred into blinding clouds by the traffic. Occasionally a vehicle slowed to a stop as the driver sought a turn-out, causing those behind to brake, bump, and raise still more dust.

It was nearly noon and pitch dark when the Gilmores reached the outskirts of Yakima and pulled into the Twin Rivers Inn. It was jammed with apprehensive motorists, drinking coffee and listening to the stream of bulletins blaring from the radio. Motorists and residents were being warned to stay inside and especially not to travel. The White Pass highway was closed. Motorists had no choice but to wait out the storm.

As they listened glumly hour after hour they learned that the huge dense cloud of ash had moved eastward, causing the Highway Patrol to close all major highways leading north, northeast, and east. The Federal Aviation Administration ordered airports shut down at Yakima, Pasco, Moses Lake, Ephrata, Ellensburg, Wenatchee, the Tri-Cities, and even Spokane, over 200 miles farther east. In these cities streetlights switched on as darkness blotted out daylight. According to new bulletins, the major eruption continued throughout the day, rising and falling in intensity but surging to new heights of 63,000 feet about 4:30 P.M. The Weather Service report stated that areas east of the volcano would experience heavy ash fallout "for an undetermined period."

By nightfall the ashfall was four inches deep from Yakima to Spokane. One man described the problem by saying, "Breathing that stuff is like sticking your head in the fireplace and stirring up the ashes." Residents were warned not to drink tap water which originated in creeks or reservoirs because of the sulfuric acid content of the ash. Schools and most businesses would be closed until further notice, and repeatedly people were advised to stay indoors. If they must venture out, they should wear protective clothing and use masks or scarves over their faces. Although all news media were flooded with calls as to whether breathing the ash was dangerous to humans or animals, no definite information was then available.

Monday morning word was received that northern Idaho and western Montana were having troubles with traffic slowdowns, heavily polluted air and water supplies, closed schools and airports. Canadian provinces reported billowing clouds of ash, as did rangers in Yellowstone National Park, and residents of northern New Mexico and eastern Wyoming.

On Tuesday the dust fell in a broad swath across the Midwest, polluting much of Nebraska, Kansas, and Oklahoma, southwestern Iowa, Missouri, and Arkansas, and neighboring Illinois, Indiana, Kentucky, Tennessee, and northern Mississippi, Alabama, and Georgia. Late that night remnants of the ashfall were recorded from New York and southward through Pennsylvania and South Carolina. Progressively, lighter amounts sifted across the Atlantic Ocean, Europe, and Asia, and seventeen days later were approaching the state of Washington from the west. Scientists predicted particles would remain in the atmosphere for at least two years or more, providing spectacular sunsets at various times and locations but not altering weather patterns.

Everybody worried about respiratory problems from breathing the volcanic ash. The Environmental Sciences Laboratory at New York's Mount Sinai School of Medicine immediately undertook a study of the ash for the U.S. National Institute of Environmental and Health Sciences. Undoubtedly there was some problem in inhaling the known silicate composition of the fragments—that is, combinations of silicon dioxide, or quartz and other impurities. Prolonged inhalation of silicates can bring on silicosis, an asthmalike disease which plagues those who work, unprotected, at sandblasting and mining.

Small wonder that Washington residents, where pollution was the heaviest, took all sorts of precautions. They cleaned out drugstores and other firms of all kinds of masks: the thin disposable ones used by doctors and nurses, the medium-strength ones designed for sufferers from hay fever and asthma, and industrial-strength ones used in cement plants, sandblasting, and coal and copper mining. Also layers of nylon hose, bandannas, and even coffee filters were used to protect humans and air systems on vehicles. So many masked persons entered banks that nervous tellers pleaded with managers to provide posters instructing customers to PLEASE REMOVE MASKS ON ENTERING. How else could they tell the difference between patrons and would-be bandits?

Stranded motorists all over central and eastern Washington, northern Idaho, and western Montana had been forced to seek shelter until traffic resumed. Schools, churches, and halls provided space to stretch out and washrooms. Residents volunteered hastily assembled meals until the air cleared enough so that Highway Patrols escorted 100-car convoys of private and commercial vehicles. On some stretches of main arterial highways drifts three- and four-feet deep had to be removed, and the shoulders were lined with abandoned cars. As always, there were those who will not cooperate for the common good. These individuals drove fast on city streets and county roads, unmindful of the dust they stirred. Some ignored roadblocks, causing accidents which added to the strain for overworked wrecker and ambulance crews. Young people who like to spin their cars and raise clouds of dust so angered bystanders that some pelted them with rocks, while others reported them to the police or sheriff's office.

Electric power had to be shut down for long periods in various communities so ash-clogged lines could be cleaned. In some towns firemen hosed ash off the main streets, swept it into mounds, and had the piles removed by front-end loaders and dumped in gullies and vacant lots.

Once it stopped "snowing" ash, people got to work with shovels and brooms. Property owners quickly learned that sweeping raised choking clouds of dust, so they tried wetting it down. Within moments they had a heavy slippery substance which defied window scrapers, brooms, and scrub brushes. Those who brushed and scraped ash off roofs found it clogged gutters and drain pipes; when swept and shoveled from yards and then hosed off the sidewalks and streets, it clogged sewers. Housewives found that countertops and glass were scratched when dusted, and only small loads of clothing could be laundered at one time, else the accumulation of muck ruined both clothing and the washing machine. Air filters on furnaces and refrigerator intakes had to be vacuumed frequently, as well as stove and furnace vents which recirculated the ash. Meanwhile, road traffic stirred up more clouds which contaminated newly cleaned objects.

Farmers faced backbreaking labor in trying to blow dust off pastures because livestock would not eat gritty forage. Dairymen dumped thousands of gallons of milk because it could not be transported to milk depots. Orchardists tried blowing, dusting with feather dusters, and spraying. Strawberry growers washed tons of gray strawberries. The ash rinsed off fairly well but the washing ruined the berries.

Clearing airport runways proved to be a gigantic undertaking, no matter how small or large the airstrip. As soon as a lane was opened, dust blown by aircraft engines on takeoff or landing settled once more into drifts. In large cities where people were dependent on bus transportation, many were late for work and appointments. At the end of the day's shift bus drivers' eyes and throats were so inflamed they needed medical treatment.

Thanks to the herculean efforts of thousands, by Thursday the Washington roads and airports were fairly functional. With main streets and parking lots partially cleared, people could get to stores and children returned to school. Amtrak's first train crossed the state—slowly. A few commercial planes landed at Spokane on a "use at your own risk" basis. Chinook Pass and White Pass were cleared for traffic, permitting travel between Yakima and Seattle and western Washington. However, all highways within the ash zone were posted "subject to closure if wind-blown ash makes driving hazardous."

A few communities promptly sought state and federal disaster relief funds. The city of Yakima found its sewage treatment plant breaking down because the lines were plugged with ash. Next, equipment used to grind larger particles malfunctioned. A call for help brought speedy assistance from Portland and Multnomah County, and Seattle and King County in the form of 12 sweepers, 8 loaders, 21 trucks, and 7 flushers. Yakima County commissioners called an emergency session, declared the city a disaster area, and sought federal funds to cover the estimated one million dollar cost for cleanup.

Lights flickered on and off in communities whose utilities received their power from Bonneville Power Administration high-voltage lines. Although the BPA quickly summoned crews for emergency repairs to the lines and transformers and substations, many had to be shut down temporarily while the equipment was swept clean. A spokesman explained that the light dry ash caused few problems, but ash dampened by the light rain which followed caused short circuits, and in some cases damaged the sophisticated equipment. Also, the light rain caused the ash resting on high-voltage lines to form a crust difficult to remove. On the other hand, a really heavy rain would have been a blessing but unfortunately the weather did not cooperate.

Still another worry mushroomed when people wondered whether or not the ash carried radioactive particles. Very soon studies were under way at the prestigious Battelle Pacific Northwest Laboratories at Richland, Washington, with its information forwarded quickly to the U.S. Environmental Agency. In layman's language, the ashfall was similar to that found in uranium mill tailings where radioactive particles decayed completely with a few hours of exposure to air. Not enough radioactive material was expelled by the volcano to cause any problems. Many of the particles were less than one micron in size, a micron being one thousandth of a millimeter. Microscopic examinations showed the particles were nontoxic but "all sharp edges," and if inhaled in large amounts over a long period could inflict respiratory problems on humans and animals.

People also worried about the damage from the ashfall being covered by comprehensive insurance. Many were reassured when representatives of several major insurance companies stated that if a driver or home owner was insured, most of the cost of repairs would be taken care of.

While an astounding amount of cleanup was accomplished in the next two weeks, farmers and orchardists had to wait months to learn whether or not the ashfall damaged their crops. The weather helped when heavy rains in June soaked the state, but it was mid-September before the tension eased as yields of near bumper size were harvested. While most farmers thought the minerals in the ash might have contributed to this, agricultural experts stated the bounty resulted from the unusual amounts of moisture.

By fall eleven study projects were being financed by National Science Foundation grants averaging about $10,000 each. Another eight studies were funded by other agencies, and twelve more were pending. The subject matter ranged from the effect of the eruption and ashfall on the white-crowned sparrow; on farmlands near Moses Lake; on which plants survived and which could be the first to grow in the mud "desert" in the disaster area; on the ant population because ants are important in wood decomposition and soil fertility; on the effect on bark beetles and woodborers; on the rate at which plants will take advantage of the minerals and nutrients of volcanic ash, and the effects of ash on the ability of plants and trees to exchange gases and retain water.

Projects not yet funded will include studies of the effects on large and small wildlife, wild birds and their habitat, the fish population, the heavy silting of the Cowlitz River estuary, and the salmon migration up the Columbia and into the Cowlitz, Toutle, and other streams now choked with logs and debris.

Nothing has been announced as yet, but studies by the Forest Service, timber companies, and USGS volcanologists undoubtedly will occupy specialists for a generation or more. At a USGS conference in Menlo Park, California, shortly after the May 18 eruption, over 150 scientists agreed that the Cascade Range offered high potential for exploiting geothermal heat as a natural source of energy. The same gigantic force which had destroyed the summit and the surrounding forests and spewed ash into the atmosphere could, in time, be harnessed by drilling into underground reservoirs for steam to run turbines. This would save on oil, natural gas, and coal now being used to produce electric power.

California is already generating commercial electricity geothermally for a city of 700,000 persons at The Geysers, 40 miles north of San Francisco. Boise, Idaho, and Klamath Falls and Lakeview in Oregon also derive a portion of their energy needs for domestic use from local geothermal sources. Other projects are under way in California's Imperial Valley, at Roosevelt Hot Springs, Utah, Valles Caldera in New Mexico, and the Puna district on the island of Hawaii. A congressional appropriation is now providing funds for research on the geothermal potentials underlying the Mount Hood volcano in Oregon. Hopefully, a similar study will be made of Mount St. Helens' future role in producing a beneficial, rather than destructive, kind of energy.

Meantime, if Mount St. Helens continued erupting for a year or two, or more, the people of Washington would just have to learn to live with volcanic ash, old and new.

7.

The Late, Great Spirit Lake

People the world over like mountains, and many cherish photographs of their favorite peak reflected in a serene blue lake surrounded by green timber. Spirit Lake, 184 feet deep and very cold, provided a mirror in which to view Mount St. Helens because it lay in a huge amphitheater facing the volcano. Alas, the peak is ugly now with that huge bite out of its north slope and its grubby ash-scarred slopes. Even if snows turn it glittering white again, it will never more be likened to an ice cream cone, or be called "Little Fujiyama."

Generations of early hunters, and Indians, and finally white men "discovered" the beautiful lake, formed when the volcano's early eruptions blocked the outlet which served as the headwaters of the Toutle River. The forest duff beneath fir, hemlock, and spruce trees around the shoreline was threaded delicately with tracks of elk, deer, bear, goats, and smaller game. The waters from a dozen rivulets of snow-melt and springs were clear and unpolluted, favored by geese and ducks, ouzels, loons, and beaver. It was the perfect summer camp for those whose pulse beat responded to nature's music, a magic place one treated with respect.

Today Spirit Lake is a mud-choked, debris-laden pond, less than half its original size, rimmed with devastated forests. Not a splintered stump remains. An unstable 100-foot-high mound of ash overran the north shore and surely will go higher if the volcano erupts again and again. Wisps of steam curl from vents which reach down to the smouldering remains of Harry Truman's lodge and his neighbors' cabins. Some future day the water may be clear again, but right now it reminds one of brown soup. At a few places one can see faint tracks of deer and coyote where confused, singed animals came to drink, turned away and never came back. The trout are dead, cooked when the water boiled. The air is sour from the "rotten egg" smell of sulfur components in the steam puffing out of the volcano's throat. There is no bird song, nor happy human sound, and the narrow highway which linked the lake to the lower Toutle valley is gone.

The Yakima Indians, who claimed the surrounding forest as their tribal hunting ground, have an interesting legend about Mount St. Helens. Briefly, it says that long before the time of man, there was a huge rock bridge spanning the great river now called the Columbia River. On top an ancient wrinkled witch, named Loo-wit, guarded the only fire in the world. Indians from north, east, south, and west came there to borrow fire. Because Loo-wit was so faithful, the Great Chief bestowed the gift of eternal life on her. This made her very unhappy and she wept, saying she did not want to be old and wrinkled forever, but young and beautiful. The Great Chief granted her wish and made her lovely again.

One day Wyeast, a handsome young chief from the land of the Multnomahs on the south side of the river, sought Loo-wit for his wife. He reached the Bridge of the Gods, as it was called, at the very moment Pahto, an ugly giant, arrived on the north shore. Pahto, too, wanted Loo-wit for his wife, so the two warriors fought bitterly, setting fire to villages and forests. The Great Chief was so angered that he crumbled the bridge into the river where the rocks formed a wild cascade. Then he smote the three lovers, but raised a mountain where each fell. Because Loo-wit was so beautiful, her mountain (St. Helens) was a dazzling white symmetrical cone. The mountain that was Wyeast lifted its head proudly (Mount Hood), while Pahto (Mount Adams) bent his head and hulking shoulders forever in sorrow as he gazed on his lost Loo-wit.

There are several versions of this legend, all written decades ago by different white men interpreting the story told them by members of the various tribes which roamed the Cascade Mountains and the shores of the Columbia River gorge. Today the Cowlitz Indians claim a close spiritual kinship with the mountain they call Lawelatla, or Person from Whom Smoke Comes. Tribal Chairman Roy Wilson feels the eruptions are caused by the spirits of ancestors protesting against white invaders who took over their hunting grounds. The Klickitat Indians call it Tah-one-lat-clah, or "Fire Mountain," with good reason. Still another legend tells of two Indian braves who were paddling across the lake in a canoe when they were swept under, and never seen again. This gave rise to the superstition that the lake was the home of demons called the Seitco or Seatco, spirits of departed chiefs who forbade the people to camp or hunt there. Yet another version states that the lake was the home of the Seatcos or Sehlatics, outcasts of several tribes because they had killed and eaten the flesh of humans.

Today white men, especially geologists, put no faith in Indian legends, either concerning the lake or the volcano. Mount St. Helens was "discovered" May 19, 1792, by Captain George Vancouver, the famed British explorer, and named Mount St. Helens in honor of an Irish peer. That peer was Alleyne Fitzherbert, Baron St. Helens, who successfully negotiated a truce with Spain in 1780 after Spanish ships seized British sailing vessels in Nootka Sound on the west coast of Vancouver Island. Contrary to popular tales, Mount St. Helens never was named for a woman or a saint.

On November 22, 1842, the volcano exploded, spewing ash over the south slope and filling small valleys extending ten miles to the Lewis River. A French-Canadian voyageur wrote at that time, "The light from the burning volcano at my cabin twenty miles away was so intense you could see to pick up a pin in the grass, at midnight."

Paul Kane, a noted pioneer Canadian artist, sketched the volcano during an eruption in March, 1847, and made these notes: "There was not a cloud visible at the time I commenced . . . suddenly a stream of white smoke shot up from the crater and hovered a short time over its summit, then settled down like a cap." The finished painting depicts two canoes with Indians viewing the fiery eruption from the middle of Spirit Lake. The original may be seen in the Royal Ontario Museum of Archaeology in Toronto, Canada.

During a quiet period in 1853 the first recorded ascent of Mount St. Helens was accomplished by a party headed by Thomas J. Dryer, founder of the Portland *Oregonian* newspaper. Since then, thousands have made their way to the summit, or skied its slopes.

Various Indians tribes used the lakeshore for their summer camps until white settlers infiltrated the region. The settlement named Toutle dates back to 1876, and a decade later logging in that area was well under way. By 1895 a logging railroad hauled timber from ten camps nearby. Nowadays one can see large clear-cut swaths, some since replanted, along Highway 504 from Toutle to Spirit Lake. There Robert C. Lange homesteaded in 1879, but real excitement developed when discoveries of shallow gold and copper ore prospects were uncovered in 1891. These led to the construction of a wagon road to the lake, and barges to transport ore across the lake to the road. Again, in 1913, something new was added, a forest fire lookout station *atop* Mount St. Helens which was then thought to be extinct, and a forest ranger station at Spirit Lake.

Although the mining soon petered out, the lakeshore drew hundreds, and later thousands, of vacationers. Since more comfortable lodgings were in demand, a family named Gustofson built a lodge one mile west of the lake and opened for business in the spring of 1929. The exact date of the addition of Harry Truman's lodge and store is debated, but it is known to have accepted guests in the early 1930s. Soon organizations established summer campgrounds along the lake, including church groups, the Portland YMCA, Portland Boy Scouts and Girl Scouts, the Longview YMCA, and others.

The first scientific study of the mountain and lake was conducted by Dr. Donald B. Lawrence of the University of Minnesota in the 1930s. Dr. Lawrence reported that a great deposit of pumice buried the region north of the volcano about 1802. Deposits of this, a hardened gray-colored volcanic glass froth, have been found twenty miles to the northwest. It is so light and porous that fragments will float like pieces of wood when thrown in the water. This same pumice provided Spirit Lake with an unusual attraction. The eruption covered trees to a depth of 12 to 20 feet. In time, the trees rotted out, leaving solid casts of their trunks called "tree wells." Those found within the Forest Service campground along the lakeshore were marked or fenced off, since the holes were hazardous to hikers and children romping about.

The 46-mile road between Castle Rock on the I-5 freeway and Spirit Lake was paved in 1946, following the completion of a large improved public campground built by the Civilian Conservation Corps. Three years later the Gifford Pinchot National Park was created, named in honor of America's first trained forester. Within another decade a road had been completed to timberline, dead-ending in a parking lot at an elevation of 4,200 feet.

For today's young readers, Spirit Lake is best known for its association with Sasquatch or Bigfoot, the huge hairy monster said to roam in small groups throughout the mountains of the Pacific Northwest. The best-known story concerns a group of gold miners who prospected the walls of a steep unnamed canyon on the northeast side of Mount St. Helens, in 1924. To protect themselves from the night cold they raised a small log shelter beside a tunnel they were boring along a gold vein. When the party ran out of fresh meat, one member went hunting for elk. Instead, he shot an enormous wild creature that stood on two feet like a human, was covered with dark hair, and even at a distance gave off an offensive odor. The wounded giant fell back off the canyon rim and its body was swept away in a swift tumbling stream a thousand feet below.

The miners retired at dark and, just before daylight, wakened when their cabin was bombarded with rocks thrown by huge hairy creatures at least seven feet tall and covered with long black hair. Frightened out of their wits by the "apes," the miners fled after the attackers left, and refused to return. Search parties organized at Longview were unable to find any trace of the hairy giants, and thereafter the scene of the attack was known as Ape Canyon.* Fifty years later the author and her husband hiked the canyon without encountering a Sasquatch, but did talk with a dozen people who had spied the creature while working in the woods on Mount St. Helens or hiking on trails leading out from Spirit Lake. Several claimed they had seen the creature on more than one occasion.

For those who might wonder if the eruption killed off any Sasquatch/Bigfoot who might have roamed the forests nearby, they may rest assured. In September several 18-inch-long, bare-toed footprints of the famed monster were discovered in the cooled ash on the north slope. Undoubtedly, more monster reports will surface in the future.

Today Spirit Lake is almost unrecognizable when compared to its former shape and beauty. When torrents of superheated mud laden with toppled trees poured into the lake shortly after the eruption, they caused a gigantic wave to race across the two-and-a-half-mile length of the lake and heated the

---

* See *On the Track of Bigfoot* by Marian T. Place, Dodd, Mead, 1974

cold water to the boiling point, cooking the fish, frogs, and other living things. The wave slammed through the narrowed lake outlet spanned by a wooden dam built during the 1920s. Greatly swollen now and churning with logs and debris, the torrent then flooded and scoured the banks of the upper Toutle River and roared on, flooding the lower valley with immense logjams and mud which eventually reached the Cowlitz River. Of the 173,000 forest acres within the St. Helens Ranger District, an estimated 156,000 acres were totally devastated. The upper half of Spirit Lake filled up as muck and ash piled 100 feet high on the north shore. Thousands of blasted trees clogged the remaining open water, now held back by a 200-foot-high plug of mud and logs, which dammed the outlet.

When the first helicopter bearing Geological Survey personnel landed at the outlet, the question immediately arose as to whether the mud plug would hold, or leak enough to drain the lake, or, without warning, would it give way and inflict another destructive flash flood on the valley below? On May 25 terror gripped the hearts of many when Mount St. Helens vented a smaller eruption, and again seventeen days later when still another occurred. The new dam held each time and appears to be stable.

However, on Wednesday, August 27, heavy rains caused an outbreak which allowed a 600-foot-wide flood to rush down the Toutle and through a Weyerhaeuser Lumber Company logging camp. While no one was injured, the new flood destroyed some heavy equipment employed in raising a containment dam near the company's Camp Baker, 15 miles west of the volcano. Weyerhaeuser had suffered severe losses in equipment following the May 18 eruption and an estimated 10 million board feet of timber in logs swept downstream into the Cowlitz and Columbia rivers. The logs were stored in a cold deck—those not sorted nor marked with the company's emblem. Alongside the cold deck at river's edge was a train made up of open-sided cars, ready to receive at least a thousand sorted and marked logs. Within 300 yards was the company office, machine shop, and parking lot lined with logging trucks and other large, heavy equipment. Twenty-four hours after the eruption the camp superintendent and a crew helicoptered into the site. It was swept clean of logs, some of the trucks wrenched askew, and some 20 feet of mud and debris burying the train and buildings. The same situation on a smaller scale had occurred at Six-Mile Camp downstream.

Numerous small gyppo or privately owned logging outfits had also lost timber and equipment, with their logs swept downstream and hopelessly tangled in the Weyerhaeuser property. Work began immediately to plow out the road into Six-Mile Camp, a slow frustrating process since the ash wore out tractor lugs, dulled blades and fouled engines. As soon as the road was open a crew and equipment of the Hamilton Construction Company of Eugene, Oregon, moved in to rebuild the railroad bridge at Six-Mile which had been torn from its footings and the girders hurtled downriver. The crew drilled through from 20 to 40 feet of ash before the bits contacted solid ground. Working three shifts, the contractor completed a temporary bridge leading across the river to the Weyerhaeuser sorting lot within eight days and proceeded to build the permanent bridge in September, two months ahead of their deadline. Not only equipment and logs had to be salvaged. The ravaged riverbed had to be cleaned of debris and a new channel excavated to handle the late fall and spring floods certain to develop when heavy rains and snowmelt caused severe runoffs from the volcano's slopes. Workmen looked upon the August 27 flood as a rehearsal for future floods. Again, within hours they were back at work, salvaging equipment and pressing to complete the containment dam by October 1, which would offer some protection to the people and land along the lower Toutle, Cowlitz, and Columbia rivers.

Every lumber outfit operating within the disaster area faces a long and costly task in rehabilitating its logging camps and sorting yards, recovering logs from stream beds and tons of ash, and salvaging downed and dying trees. Loggers labor in a tangled graveyard of uprooted trees and splintered stumps, all that is left of 300-year-old prime mature Douglas fir and hemlock.

One logger working inside the blast zone explained, "These trees are half-cooked from heat."

Asked if he and his fellow workmen had been evacuated during working hours, he replied, "Yes, more than once. We also have to quit work when the wind is from the east and blows ash down on us. We wear protective masks. When it rains, the ash turns to mud and balls up under our corks [boots], making footing very dangerous. But the work has to go on. Some of these trees have developed blue stain already, a fungus that kills them but doesn't make them useless for construction or plywood, or pulp."

As great as the damage is, Weyerhaeuser Company experts discovered after studies were completed that the company actually lost more timber from its holdings in the area following a major forest fire in 1902 and again in 1962 when the region was lashed with tornado-strength winds which flattened acres of timberland on Columbus Day. At least much of the devastated timberland is harvestable on its 473,000-acre St. Helens Tree Farm. However, 25,000 of these acres contained trees too young to cut or salvage. These must be removed quickly to prevent their becoming a fire hazard and to make room for new seedlings. Experimental replantings in test plants began in June with seedlings placed in three different plots: one containing 6 to 8 inches of volcanic ash, a second into a mixture of half ash and half soil, and a third where the ash was scraped away and the young plants set down in soil. Six months later those planted in soil appeared to be doing the best.

In December heavy rains not only washed out the containment dam on the North Toutle but a second one placed closer to the volcano. Once more a surge of water, mud, and debris flooded the river. Thanks to the emergency warning systems set up, no humans or livestock were injured, though some ranches fell victim to partial flooding. As the alert was radioed to the Army Corps of Engineers, their dredges were moved at once to new positions at the mouth of the Cowlitz so the ship channel in the Columbia River would not silt up again. Afterward people expressed satisfaction with the results. If they could not control the volcano or the weather, at least they were learning the hard way how to minimize future losses.

Still, no one dares think too optimistically at this time about what future eruptions and severe seasonal flooding will do to the late, great Spirit Lake.

8.

More Eruptions, More Problems

Nothing has been said at length about the courageous work of Geological Survey geologists, geophysicists, and volcanologists, and a host of others from universities and scientific organizations after the May 18 eruption. Stories about destruction, death, and search and rescue captured the headlines. Yet within hours that Sunday a small corps of scientists and civilian aides began replacing the monitoring instruments destroyed in the blast and pyroclastic flow. True, these men could have waited until Mount St. Helens calmed down before venturing out, but to do so would have been a disservice to volcanology. Relying on seismographs installed at distant stations would have provided too little information.

Seismographs do not record surface temperatures nor the degrees of heat at various levels under the steaming floor, nor the temperatures and composition of a dead lake, nor gather and analyze samples of ash, nor record gravity and magnetic changes, nor test streams for acids and solids, nor describe drastic changes in the new crater. All this valuable information is essential not only in accumulating new data on the day-to-day behavior of a live volcano. It also furnishes clues as to whether or not the volcano is approaching another eruption, so people within range of its destructive force can be evacuated. The volcano has much to reveal to scientists who dare assault the quivering, steaming slopes and crater. Thus, these specialists and the pilots who transported them safely to and from hazardous areas deserve our respect.

Before the May 18 eruption ceased, Lon Stickney, chief pilot for the Geological Survey, was ordered to pick up scientists at Vancouver and search the mountain for David Johnston, reported missing on Coldwater Ridge. Knowing it would be a dangerous flight, the pilot first checked out the target area. "At Coldwater where I thought Dave would be, the trees were blown down to bare rock and the trailer was gone. I could see explosions going on along the upper Toutle. There were no trees left standing, and where there'd been a valley before, now there were small mountains of volcanic material. I became so emotionally distraught I could not report in on the radio."

On the trip, with every seat in the five-passenger Bell 206 helicopter loaded, Stickney flew the upwind side of the steam eruption. "I could get pretty close. The only thing holding me back was those huge chunks of ice being shot in the air. The noise of the blades turning made conversation impossible, so no one was talking. We were pretty certain Dave was gone."

The next day Stickney lifted personnel onto the slopes, and the shoreline of Spirit Lake. They installed new instruments, took readings, collected samples, and surveyed the appalling changes. The geologists had unlimited air access to the volcano, as did the search craft, but others had to obtain clearances, which sometimes took a while and angered news photographers. On Wednesday Stickney carried on his work in spite of winds which reached 45 miles per hour and rain clouds. Finally, as fog rolled in, he picked up everyone and returned to the airport. With almost daily flights since then, barring bad weather, he has logged more hours over St. Helens than any other pilot.

Dr. Peter Rowley was one of three geologists studying the pyroclastic flows, and during quiet periods went down into the crater. Even during a "quiet" period the volcano belched steam and gas from various vents on its floor, and now and then tossed out a few rocks. "It was eerie. You could see the steam billowing over the lip, and know there'd be no way you could get out fast enough if you needed to. Your first time going into the crater, you're looking every which way. After a bit you forget about it because you're so excited about what you're observing and learning."

A companion, Mel Kuntz, agreed. "The first day inside is scary. You have shaky knees, but you get over it. It's dangerous work, but we have good pilots and we'd have a warning if real trouble was developing." Another geologist, Norman MacLeod, stressed, "The pilots are with us all the time. They hover as close as they can and keep their blades going. Flying inside those steep crater walls is always very risky."

When asked where the warnings could originate, these men explained that everyone working in the crater wore a walkie-talkie and thus was in constant touch with the command center at Vancouver. Its staff kept in touch with the pilots who, simultaneously, were in touch with the dispatch center, the patrol plane flying above them, and radioed, up-to-the-minute reports from the Weather Service.

Since geologists do most of their work outdoors, they wear hiking boots, jeans, and wool shirts instead of white laboratory coats. While the surface of the unstable pyroclastic flow cooled, the subsurface registered temperatures up to 330° Celsius (626° F) for days after the eruption. Lisa McBroome, one of the women Survey geologists working on the volcano unfortunately stepped into some soft, very hot material and suffered second-degree burns on her legs. Others discovered the soles of their heavy boots almost burned through.

Much of the work took place outside the crater and included measuring the depth of the pyroclastic flows at varying locations between the northern "lip" and Spirit Lake. Long spikes were pounded into rocks at the edge of the crater, the theory being that the amount of spike remaining exposed after the next eruption would reveal the amounts of ash flung out in a new flow. A few individuals were involved in mapping the drastically altered landscape, even though they would have to repeat their measurements whenever St. Helens spewed out additional deposits of ash and debris.

Mel Kuntz explained the need for immediate mapping. "Flows are easily eroded. A year from now some will be washed away or covered with younger material. Right now we're trying to get as much done as possible before winter weather and deep snow put a halt to work for weeks. There's still lots to be done on lower levels below timberline, this year and for lots of years ahead."

Although Ken Yamashita grew up with volcanoes in Hawaii, he found Mount St. Helens an unusually eerie place to work. Along with Gene Iwatsubo, he worked with an electronic distance-measuring device which bounces laser beams off reflectors located around the volcano in order to detect any swelling or shrinking in the slopes. Before May 18 the north slope was swelling more than five feet daily, yet in October the rate was less than half an inch daily. According to Donald Peterson, scientist in charge of the USGS Mount St. Helens project after Mullineaux and Crandell returned to Denver, "Those figures total more than twelve feet a year. That's fast, in geologic time, but not alarming." He, too, had worked on Hawaii's volcanoes but felt safe enough while working near St. Helens' crater. "As long as we have radio contact and are kept fully informed, we're comfortable."

One of the stations on the volcano used by helicopters is called Harry's Ridge, in memory of Harry Truman, the crusty resort owner who died in the May 18 blast. Pilots named it while trying to find a recognizable landmark. Stumps of large fir trees sheared off that day mark the location.

Civilians not schooled as scientists were then, and still are, employed in various ways on the volcano's flanks. Laurence Loree and Robert Bradshaw of Chehalis, both in their fifties, were assigned a chilly and spooky task. They drew the all-night volcano watch at Spirit Lake. Each had his own pickup truck and shortwave radio. They were instructed to radio the alarm to the volcano watch headquarters at Vancouver if the dam started to give way, and then leave as speedily as possible. They didn't have to wait long for action.

On Sunday morning, May 25, at 2:39 A.M. Mount St. Helens suddenly roared to life, erupting a plume of steam and ash which, they learned later, soared 43,000 feet high. The two reported in and then dashed for safety. Later they told reporters the explosions were bright and colorful, with lots of vivid orange and pale yellow reflecting from the cone onto the clouds and down to where they were. "The thunder near rattled our bones. It was like a million little explosions and then a big boom. Right away came the ash. It sounded like sleet hitting our trucks, and was pure white in the headlights."

The eruption lasted seven hours. The plume was caught in strong winds at varying levels: those at 12,000 feet blew the ash toward Longview and Kelso, which received ashfall from one to three inches deep; those at 24,000 feet whisked a fine coating of ash as far north as Olympia and southward onto Portland and Salem, Oregon; winds still higher swept the ash along the Pacific Coast. However, this time the ash was mixed with light rain, forming a slippery slush. Once more airlines suspended flights, private and commercial traffic on highways was shut down, and electrical transformers damaged. By 4:00 A.M. mudballs fell over the Longview-Kelso area and at 7:00 A.M. it was still as dark as night. All search-and-rescue flights were canceled. Residents of Cougar and Yale, ten miles southwest of the volcano, already had been evacuated in orderly convoys and arrived safely at Battle Ground where the Red Cross had set up a shelter and provided cots, blankets, coffee, and soft drinks. A reporter interviewed the refugees as they registered. When Mrs. Alice Merkel was asked if she was surprised at having to evacuate, she shifted her two-year-old son on her hip and replied, "No, we've had a bag packed all week."

When helicopter crews stationed at Toledo were alerted, they dressed hurriedly and raced outside. Crew Chief Deborah Beck reported, "I ran out and covered that bird with everything from paper sacks to plastic bags, and got most of the major components covered OK." Had the engines been started in response to emergency summonses, the muddy mixture would have been drawn into the power plants, causing the engines to fail moments later while in flight. Fortunately, none were needed until the air cleared.

Tim Hait, spokesman for the U.S. Geological Survey, sounded a positive note. "This new ashfall may be a sign that much of the pressure building up within the volcano was released. We may be darned lucky we have St. Helens clearing its throat this way once in a while, rather than staging another huge blowup." Hait also revealed that a number of scientists, including Dr. Dwight R. Crandell, volcano-hazards coordinator for the USGS, had spent much of Saturday on the topmost flanks of the volcano and had seen nothing to indicate there would be another eruption hours later.

By late afternoon Sunday, electrical power outages had been corrected and once more people resumed the gritty cleanup in the old and new areas. It was a monumental task, since highway officials estimated 26,000 miles of roadway in central and eastern Washington were made impassable by the May 18 ashfall, and another 2,000 miles by the new eruption. Two companies of guardsmen from the Seattle-Tacoma area of the 181st Support Battalion of the Army National Guard, numbering over 1,000 men, assisted in the removal of millions of tons of ash, but most small areas had to dig themselves out.

In Yakima officials contacted Chuck Hardacre of Power

Master, Inc. of Portland, and leased six Vactors, high-powered vacuum cleaners costing $160,000 each, to suck the gritty ash off roofs and out of sewer lines. These ran in 12-hour shifts, with the last two hours of each shift spent in washing, greasing, and refueling the machines. In two days one machine vacuumed seventeen tons of ash off the roof of the City Hall. Hardacre reported his crews cleaned an average of 110 to 113 catch basins during each shift. To the few who complained about the cost of using the Vactors, he replied, "Think how long it would take a man with a shovel to pick up the ash and load it onto a dump truck." When the city's sewer treatment plant shut down because ash clogged the lines, the Vactors cleaned out the plant's digesters and clarifiers. Still, during the shutdown the Yakima River became dangerously contaminated with raw sewage and all residents were forced to purchase bottled water or boil water for personal use.

Unfortunately, as soon as roads were passable, drivers ignored the 10-mile-per-hour speed limit and drove at high speeds, grinding the troublesome ash into finer particles. The Environmental Protection Agency (EPA) warned drivers repeatedly to observe more reasonable speeds. Spokesman Robert Jacobson stated, "Washington drivers are recirculating air pollution, and creating air-quality problems that can last for months." At various locations highway patrolmen reported almost "blizzardlike" conditions from ash being whipped into the air, limiting visibility, causing accidents, and surrounding motorists with particles that could cause respiratory diseases. Being cited for speeding and having to pay fines had little effect on the violators. A headline in *The Seattle Times* described the I-5 freeway between Portland and Seattle as "a zoo with rear-enders. Raindrops full of 'mash'—a mixture of mud and ash—collected on the windshields of passing cars, smearing it into a brown mask as the wipers moved the goop around with virtually no effect."

Relatives of missing persons still harangued deputies and guardsmen for permission to conduct private searches. After all, they said, they'd lived all their lives in the region and wouldn't get lost. The difficulty was that the areas they knew so well no longer existed. They were buried under mountains of ash and debris, and a man plodding through that material barely averaged more than a few miles a day. It did not seem to occur to these individuals that because they were not trained for search-and-rescue missions and lacked proper equipment and clothing, they, too, might have to be rescued, thereby adding to the already heavy burden on crews and equipment.

A grim note, yet one softening the blow for the survivors of blast victims, came from Dr. John Eisele, a King County medical examiner. After completing autopsies on the four members of the Siebold family and Fred and Margery Rollins, he stated, "They appeared to have died painlessly, overcome by still-unidentified toxic gases emitted by the volcano May 18. There are some burns, but no blast or explosion-type injuries. It appears to have been asphyxial, more like smoke inhalation from a house fire." Later he added that although he had studied his pathology reference text, a comprehensive collection of what authorities know about the causes of death, "there is not one word which applies to victims of volcanic eruptions. So, now we write a new chapter."

Still another aftermath came to light when Hugh Homan, entomologist from the University of Idaho, completed a study of orchard damage in the Yakima area, where 15 percent of the nation's crop of red and golden Delicious apples are grown. He warned that severe outbreaks of the spider mite, an insect that attacks foliage, could develop. The mite is usually kept under control by other insects, but now, because of the ash, the mite-devouring predators were smothered.

Then, Dr. Carl Johansen, a Washington State University entomologist, revealed that 12,000 bee colonies, or 17 percent of the state's total commerical production, had been severely damaged or wiped out by the ashfall. One beekeeper explained, "We have to decide whether to keep the colonies together to give them a chance to generate some honey, or split them into smaller colonies to have enough to take to California. Normally we do move them during the winter to pollinate crops and increase our hives, but splitting them makes them weaker and more susceptible to injury. For many, our future as beekeepers is very iffy."

Every time the mountain jiggled, rumors spread like particles of ash. The two most unsettling rumors were that the dam, or mud plug, at Spirit Lake was weakening, and the oil and natural gas lines buried under the Toutle River had cracked, causing gas to build up and threaten a terrific explosion. Thanks to the enterprising reporters, the rumors were checked out, and most laid to rest. So far, the newly formed dam blocking Spirit Lake appeared to be stable. Water was trickling out from under the dam, leaching out small material, but this caused larger rocks to settle and fit together closer, strengthening the dam. Geologists had to assure the public that the dam would not slide downhill, and if the lake rose to the top of the dam, it would pour over and find its way downstream without a catastrophic flood. Logjams and barriers of debris scattered downstream would halt the runoff.

However, Dr. Crandell of the USGS reminded residents of the Cowlitz River valley, which includes Longview and Kelso, that they faced possible severe flooding even if the natural dam at Spirit Lake held, and the volcano did no further damage. The tons of mud which poured into the Toutle and Cowlitz created a new riverbed 15 feet higher than normal. Even the usual fall and winter rains could erode the ash-strewn flanks of the volcano severely, and another round of mudflows could once again imperil those streams, possibly the Kalama River and Yale Reservoir on the Lewis River.

As for the natural gas and oil pipelines crossing under the Toutle, tests showed they had withstood both the tremors and overburden of debris, and were operating normally. So much for that rumor.

Another tale concerned the 5 million yearling coho salmon reared at the state hatchery at Mayfield Dam on the Cowlitz. In normal years the prize crop was released into the Cowlitz. Now, supposedly, the fish were going to be released into the mud-choked Cowlitz where they would turn belly up. Fishermen declared their taxes helped pay to rear the salmon, so why couldn't they come to the hatchery and scoop up a creel or two? The answer was that the year's plantings had been moved by tank trucks to the Columbia River and released far enough upstream to avoid the polluted water.

Midweek after the big bang some fish biologists declared the eruption and mudflows had rendered the Toutle and Cowlitz barren of fish for possibly 100 years. Water temperatures had reached such high levels for such a long time that no fish could have survived, and this also affected fishing on the Columbia downstream because of the outflow of silt.

Recreationists' vehicles trapped by trees on Weyerhaeuser land near Green River bridge about 12 miles north of the volcano.

Loggers have gone back to work, but they wear devices to measure the amount of volcanic dust inhaled during work shift.

The Columbian, Cheryl Haselhorst

The volcano's devastation is evident at St. Helens Lake.

Meta Lake, surrounded by blasted-down trees, is approximately seven miles northeast of Mount St. Helens.

Chunks of ice thrown out by the eruption eventually melt and form "kettles." Volcanologist Donal Mullineaux collects samples.

Dedication of Ridgefield Exit Volcano Information Center, July 4, 1980.

Worse, since migrating salmon were said to return to their native streams, those hatched in the Cowlitz and Toutle would die before spawning.

Surprisingly, by late August the State Game Department fish biologists were finding a large number of summer-run steelhead trout had avoided the Cowlitz and bypassed instead into the clear Kalama River nearby. Biologist Bob Watson pointed out, "In any group or race of fish, you have a certain amount of straying. I think this is nature's way of accomodating natural disasters. Fish are remarkably tenacious. They'll hang on in unbelievable situations."

Bill Rees, head of natural salmon production for the State Fisheries Department, reported well over half the natural spawning areas in the Cowlitz and Toutle and the latter's tributaries were destroyed. "In places near the mountain the Toutle flows underground. We don't know what will happen when the rains come in October and November. Maybe they will wash the ash down the hillsides into the rivers and cause still more problems."

This did happen to some extent, but not as badly as feared, yet will continue to imperil spawning beds for years to come.

In an effort to save the genetic stock of fish until those rivers can be rehabilitated, efforts are being made to provide private financing to rear 20,000 young Toutle River steelhead in ponds on Salmon Creek, near Vancouver. The adult steelhead which produced these juveniles had been transferred as part of the management program preceding Mount St. Helens' eruption.

The second eruption heightened problems of a different nature to the small communities of Cougar and Toutle. Since these towns had received more national news coverage than

123

others in the region, postmasters there were swamped with requests from all over the United States for mail cancellations, beginning with the March 27 eruption. According to Cougar Postmaster Alice Thomas, "One school class sent decorated envelopes and asked me to postmark them on the date of the big eruption. Fortunately, I had in stock a good supply of stamped postcards, and once the volcanic activity got really going, they sold out. Before the big bang we had set up a pickup service for about thirty customers cut off by the road blockades in dangerous areas. We also had to handle increasing loads of mail for the St. Helens Ranger Station."

Both postmasters in the two mountain towns are women, as are the contract mail carriers. Judy Whitmore works the route from Woodland through Cougar, and delivers mail to those who live at the foot of the volcano. "My route was shortened when the Forest Service and some other families evacuated. Now it ends just two miles east of Cougar. Yes, I'm aware of the dangers but people around here don't get too upset about the volcano. My job is to deliver the mail, and as long as it's possible, I will."

On Wednesday, May 28, Governor Ray warned the people of Washington that they must be prepared for more eruptions because the volcano was still unstable. While the state division of health had determined there was no major health hazard from the ash covering much of the state, individuals exposed to the most recent and future fallouts should wear protective face masks. The health division was in the process of establishing surveillance systems for respiratory problems at hospitals in Cowlitz, Clark, Benton, Whitman, Spokane, Yakima, and Grant counties.

In her fifteen-minute television broadcast Governor Ray gave the people some idea of how many agencies were involved in post-eruption problems:

Social and Health Services were monitoring air quality and establishing emergency assistance offices to aid low income and displaced families. Inmate labor from prison honor camps was available to help in the ash cleanup.

Office of Employment Security was making available unemployment compensation benefits for workers left jobless because of the eruption. Provisions had been made for more than 100 Comprehensive Employment and Training Act (CETA) workers to assist in the Yakima cleanup, and another 100 in Spokane.

Agriculture agencies were assessing crop damage and expediting delivery of emergency livestock feed. Loan assistance was now available for low-income farmers.

State Highway Patrol announced roadside assistance and traffic control duties during the emergency so far had resulted in the loss of about 25 percent of the vehicle fleet, and replacements would cost an estimated $2 million.

Department of Ecology was monitoring sewage and wastewater systems in afflicted areas.

National Guard still had 1,500 guardsmen on active duty to help search-and-rescue teams and clean-up squads. To date, more than 350 search missions had been conducted since May 18.

Emergency Services personnel were coordinating all state emergency operations through offices in Vancouver and Olympia (the state capital).

While all this information served to assure residents that their tax-supported agencies were working on their behalf, it also served to enlighten them about the large and varied services called into action on behalf of all those affected in one way or another by the volcano's action.

In other words, Mount St. Helens' eruptions already were the most costly shows on earth, and return engagements were a certainty.

9.

The mighty Columbia Is Plugged

Twenty-two hours after the May 18 eruption Captain John Satalich, a skilled river pilot, was guiding the *Hoegh Mascot,* a Norwegian freighter, eastward up the Columbia River toward Longview, Washington. At 5:05 A.M., just before dawn, he realized his ship was no longer moving. There had been no sharp jolt nor loud scraping noise, nor had he expected any, since, according to his navigational map, the *Hoegh Mascot* was proceeding in an orderly manner in the 40-foot-deep channel. Yet somehow it had shoaled and wasn't budging one inch.

Immediately Captian Satalich radioed the U.S. Coast Guard and the corpsman-dispatcher called Adam J. Heineman, chief of the navigation division of the North Pacific, U.S. Army

Corps of Engineers at Portland. For a moment Heineman wondered if he had received a crank call. Ships just don't run
aground in the middle of a channel which the Corps kept
dredged deep enough to accomodate ocean-going vessels.
Then he remembered Mount St. Helens had erupted the morning before and, according to the radio, the North Toutle carried thousands of logs, tons of debris, and untold quantities
of mud into the Cowlitz, and within hours the Cowlitz dis-
gorged the treacherous burden into the Columbia, south of
Longview. The mighty Columbia—broad, swift, very powerful,
second mightiest of the nation's rivers—was plugged. Worse,
twenty or more vessels ready to depart the inland port of
Portland, others berthed at Vancouver and Longview, and
as many more heading upstream were entrapped.

Heineman's first move was to dispatch a survey ship to
take soundings of the channel depth, normally 40-feet deep
and 600-feet wide in the critical area above and below
Longview. The word went out for all traffic to cease until
soundings were completed. Captains and crews waited and
waited, because the water was so loaded with silt that sonar
equipment on the survey ship could not register any readings.
A helicopter equipped with weighted lines was summoned,
and for the first time in thirty years of channel work, the
Corps used weighted lines to determine channel depths. The
figures were dismaying. For five miles in either direction from
the point where the Cowlitz empties into the Columbia, the
channel was only 17-feet deep.

Next, calls were made to dredging contractors in the region.
Two days passed before the first arrived, the *Pacific,* once
used to dredge Okinawa's ports during World War II but
now engaged in clearing Oregon's small fishing harbors. *Pacif-*

ic's Captain Ernest McReynolds was appalled. "This is the worst I have seen in my twenty-three years of dredging."

When newsmen clamored for information, they learned the *Pacific* was a hopper dredge which crept along, self-propelled, at one knot per hour with two drag-arms extending down from each side to suck up water, sand, and rock slurry. A 340-horsepower pump moved the slurry into four open bins where the water was filtered out and the sediment collected. When the bins were full, the drag-arms were retracted, the *Pacific* chugged to a designated dumping area, the hopper doors opened, and the sludge was dumped back into the river or along the shore. Then the dredge returned to its area and repeated the process, each cycle consuming 40 minutes.

After two more hopper dredges arrived, and within six days, the three cleared a 200-foot-wide channel which attained a depth of 30 feet during high tide. The twice-daily, two-hour periods called "high-tide windows" enabled most of the entrapped ships to get under way, one at a time, up or downstream. The problem was far from solved. Three pipeline dredges were added to widen the channel another 400 feet.

On May 23 three vessels outbound from Portland inched through the "window" between noon and 1:00 P.M. These included an aluminum ore carrier, a container ship, and a general cargo vessel. During the second hour in the "window," one ship incoming from Astoria got through safely. But 24 freighters were holding at Astoria-at the mouth of the Columbia, still unable to proceed upriver.

The following week dredging crews lowered the channel to 35 feet, and 15 U.S. Navy vessels reached Portland to participate in the city's annual Festival of Roses. Still, vessels with a draft of more than 13 feet were banned from transiting the plugged segment. This included 19 upriver and 14 naval and other vessels undergoing repairs at Portland's huge Swan Island complex. Finally, to assist in hurrying along the dredging, the Port of Portland dispatched its huge dredge because the city's grain elevators would be filled within days by shipments from upriver, and thus be unable to accept additional wheat shipments until traffic resumed. Alerted that grain shipments which require more than a 30-foot channel could be delayed as much as five months, and to prevent an accumulation of grain cars in the railroad yards, the Burlington Northern and Union Pacific placed embargoes on export shipments of all commodities bound for Portland, Vancouver, and Kalama.

In spite of this frantic round-the-clock effort, the Columbia remained virtually closed to the heaviest freighters, which could not negotiate the "windows." This drastically affected the shipping tonnage, since many vessels which did pass through had to load only to half-capacity and return empty. Hundreds of longshoremen found themselves unemployed and newly completed facilities at Portland remained unoccupied. The latter created a loss of $4 million daily in income. When newspapers and shipping trade journals announced that the May 18 eruption caused 51 million cubic yards of volcanic muck—enough to fill one-quarter of the Panama Canal—to raise the Columbia's channel, many ship owners sought berths in other coastal ports. The fact that the Corps of Engineers was employing 300 men and six dredges at a cost of $44 million to clear the plug did not assure owners that a similar delaying situation would not develop every time a major eruption occurred in the future. Eventually taxpayers would pay the cost of the cleanup and unemployment compensation for more than 700 longshoremen, all because a long-sleeping volcano came awake.

The more shallow channel had little effect on pleasure craft and fishing vessels but the debris, particularly tumbling logs and portions of torn bridges and structures, played havoc with marinas and houseboats along the shoreline. At Kelso cranes were brought in to salvage 75 boats resting lopsidedly amidst the debris. Native and hatchery-bred fish and migratory birds also suffered when the muck flooding their natural habitats dried to cementlike consistency. Possibly the muck dredged from the channel will be used to create extensions to present and even new islands now serving as wildlife nesting refuges.

Mel Gordon, chairman of the Pacific Northwest River Basin Commission, announced nine of twenty-seven research contracts for studying the Columbia River estuary would receive $20,000 each for extra personnel and gear, in order to study the effects of the sediment and debris accumulated in the estuary. Logs—some of which traveled from the timbered slopes of the volcano—were causing severe scouring of the life-supporting estuarine marshes, upsetting the delicate food chain for bottom-feeding species. Also, toxic chemicals released from loosened bark created another danger to estuarine flora and fauna. The dense mud barrier could cause juvenile salmon to starve, or force them prematurely to start their life-threatening journey to the open sea.

Due to the all-out effort to repair the damage, by fall ship traffic was approaching normal. But dredges and crews labored on through 18-hour shifts because of the very real danger which could develop when late fall and winter rains caused drastic flooding of pyroclastic material off St. Helens' slopes and forced more logjams down the Toutle and Cowlitz.

A Survey geologist reminded those who would be affected by future flooding, "These are facts we have to accept and fit into our future. Clearing the streams of logs, deepening and widening channels will help, but there's always the unknown, the future eruptions clouding the future."

10.

The Explosive Phase Continues

indful that Mount St. Helens erupted violently two Sundays in a row, people worried that it would release a third superheated jet on Sunday, June 1. Instead, behaving like a child exhausted after a severe tantrum, the volcano sulked, hiccoughing steam and gas quietly. Though needles on seismographs jiggled, geologists were relieved when earthquake activity and harmonic tremors dropped to a low level.

Tim Hait, Geological Survey spokesman, explained at a press briefing, "St. Helens is still in a highly explosive state. We like to see gases coming out, rather than blocking up, which increases the potential for explosion. The glowing hot spots in the crater are surface rocks heated to an estimated 900 degrees Fahrenheit by gases emitted from molten rock moving far below."

133

Survey personnel had placed more tiltmeters on the volcano and reset targets for laser measurements of the ravaged surface. Meteorologists reported ash hurtled into the stratosphere May 18 had completed the around-the-world journey and was back over North America, but creating no atmospheric problems. Intermittent showers helped reduce air pollution levels and made working at ground level amidst ash-strewn debris slippery but less dusty. In time, specialists said, the ash would work its way into the soil, or be buried in landfills or pack down, except where it lay in deep drifts on the slopes and around Spirit Lake. Nevertheless, the people of Washington State faced a long and costly cleanup, especially in the region east of the Cascades where summer heat is accompanied by gusty winds. Housewives resigned themselves to a continuing battle with dust.

During the quiet spell headlines focused on a Seattle-based film crew that broke the law, and paid dearly for it. When the volcano subsided after its March 27 eruption, Otto Sieber, forty-two, and four aides slipped past barricades into the high-danger "red" zone, climbed to the summit and part way down into the crater to obtain exclusive photographs. The fact that all returned safely whetted their desire for a second venture. In spite of knowing the penalty for violating the restrictions was a $1000 fine and five years in jail, they climbed the slope again on May 24 and slept out overnight.

When the volcano erupted the next day, they were high enough to suffer from intense heat, violent winds, tremors, and falling hot debris. Miraculously, they survived and painfully stumbled down the mountain in the murky light and choking dust. The next morning a search helicopter crew spied their distress signals and transported them to a hospital. Frightened, eyes almost swollen shut, hair singed, exposed skin scorched, bruised by falling, they were a sorry sight. The search crew alerted the Skamania County sheriff, who promptly charged them under a 1979 state law giving him the authority to close areas where search-and-rescue missions were being carried on. Later the county prosecutor served them with a writ to appear September 15 in the county Superior Court to face charges of illegal trespassing. As the prosecutor said, "Their conduct was irresponsible and endangered lives—their own and their rescuers."

Incredibly, publicity about Sieber's crew did not discourage Mark Perry, thirty-eight, of Spokane and James Standiford, thirty-seven, of Newman Lake from breaching the barricades and spending ten days photographing Spirit Lake and its steaming slopes. Only when Standiford seriously injured a leg in a fall did Perry signal distress by using a mirror. Asked why they risked their lives, Perry exclaimed, "This is the story of the century! I can't figure how come everyone isn't going in there. If Jim hadn't injured his leg, we had grub enough to stay another week." Neither revealed how they avoided being spotted by search-and-rescue squads, who would have removed them forcibly from the area.

Beginning May 28, loggers resumed operations at Twelve Road, a Weyerhaeuser camp between the forks of the Toutle and 20 miles from the crater. Not all workers reported, preferring to subsist on unemployment compensation of about $137 a week, approximately the sum they earned per day when working. Others facing car, house, and insurance payments of $900 or more each month felt obligated to report, even though they feared the volcano. Superintendents of several outfits which resumed logging no longer relied on geologists' opinions that their workers would have up to two hours to evacuate after an eruption. That estimate had been based on the rate lava flows would move down the slopes. But St. Helens had spilled no lava as yet, so evacuation plans were altered to cope with the possibility of more pyroclastic flows and gigantic mudslides.

The first day back on the job was devoted to orientation to the new and hazardous working conditions and faster evacuation procedures. Now vans and pickups, formerly used to transport two to three crews into remote and separated logging areas, were assigned one to each crew for a speedier exit. Supervisors and crew chiefs were equipped with two-way radios, providing communication among all crews and up-to-the-minute volcano reports. Masks were supplied by the employers, since the men must work in heavy ash stirred up as logs were loaded. None of these crews worked in areas devastated by the May 18 blast. Only volunteer squads of five to six men moved cautiously into the high-danger zone to salvage large expensive equipment and trucks. These men were provided two-way radios, masks, food and water, and instructed to move out immediately at the first warning of danger.

People's anxiety lessened when Sunday, June 1, passed quietly on the volcano. Two days later a high-intensity harmonic tremor, similar to those preceding the May 18 and May 25 eruptions, rumbled within the peak. Evacuation orders crackled over the air waves, and all woodsworkers, Survey crews, and search-and-rescue squads attained a safe staging area when the mountain roared and hurtled a steam plume 14,000 feet into the air.

Once more, reporters clamored for information. One asked

Tim Hait, "What about a tiltmeter recording an increase in the ground elevation on the south side of the mountain in the Ape Cave area?" The cave was one of several damp lava tubes which were touted falsely as possible hiding places used by the Bigfoot/Sasquatch monsters.

Hait answered that the increase in elevation was very minor, averaging only one microradian a day.

"What's a *microradian?*" the reporter demanded, checking on the spelling and pronunciation.

"A microradian is an angular measurement which corresponds to an elevation increase of one millimeter," the Survey spokesman explained patiently. By comparison, a tiltmeter placed on the north side bulge prior to May 18 recorded increases of 300 microradians every fifteen minutes.

"Does the increase on the south side mean it is going to bulge and blow out like the north side?"

The only answer Hait could provide was, "We don't know. We have to wait and see."

For the moment the news media persons were satisfied. They had a bit of news, a new term *microradian* to brighten their dispatches, and a chance to infer that maybe—but maybe not—the south side posed a threat and another great eruption was in the works.

Those who lived south of the volcano and along the Lewis River and its three huge reservoirs had escaped damage so far, except for a liberal dusting, and carried on as normally as possible. They stocked up on food and bottled water and seldom strayed far from their radios. After the May 25 eruption all who lived near the head of Swift Reservoir, only eight miles below the crater, evacuated hastily. When a search squad made a house-to-house check, they found only Ray

Jennings, seventy-five, who lived alone in a small neat cabin. When the men pleaded with him to leave, he refused politely. No need to, he declared. All the activity was on the other side of the volcano. The morning of May 18 he heard the big boom, and climbed the high ridge between his place and the peak in order to watch the big show. "When I returned to my cabin, I put a glass of water on the counter and watched it shake. It danced all day! But I was all right, and so was my place. I couldn't see any sense in leaving. The next day was worse because it rained ash and was as dark as midnight all day. I couldn't get any television or radio programs, so I just took it easy and read. Some of my neighbors had abandoned their dogs and I fed them along with my own four. Couple days later some Army fellows come down in a helicopter and was going to make me leave. My niece in Portland had told them I could live with her 'til things quieted down. I told those fellows I wasn't going to leave. I had plenty of propane and a six-month supply of food. I told them to tell my niece to quit worrying. They finally left."

But people continued to worry about the gentle old man. On May 30, Thomas McDowell, fire chief of the nearby settlement of Yacolt, flew in and finally persuaded Jennings to leave. He agreed, provided all the dogs accompanied him. "Might as well go," he conceded a little grumpily. "That volcano sure ruined my summer."

During the lull thousands of sightseers jammed the I-5 freeway and roads within the forest which were open to the public. The first weekend that an Information Center, housed in a small trailer, was set up by the Forest Service on a parking lot alongside the Yale Reservoir, 10,000 visitors overwhelmed the staff with questions. The Forest Service announced two additional Information Centers would be opened by July 4, one at the Ridgefield Exit (Number 14) on Interstate 5 north of Vancouver, and another off Exit 68 at Lewis and Clark State Park on the Jackson Highway north of Toledo. Both sites provided unobstructed views of the steaming volcano and parking spaces for a large number of vehicles. Inside the Visitors Centers, housed in double-wide, 56-foot-long trailers, would be five rangers assigned to answer questions, a small room for viewing a brief colored film of the volcano before, during, and after the May 18 eruption, a seismograph for viewers to observe, and an exhibit of wall-size photographs. Since there would be no admission fee, possibly four million visitors would pass through the Centers during the summer and fall.

Despite the threat of more eruptions clouding their future, there was little of the "gloom-and-doom" defeatist attitude among those whose lives were changed by the eruption. One major factor was that insurance companies would be paying over $11.7 million in damage claims because the eruption was classified as an "explosion." The losses would not have been covered if the eruption had been interpreted as an earthquake, and almost no policy holders considered earthquake coverage necessary for their area. When the author interviewed members of families who had suffered property damage, they replied, "We're not pulling out. Lots of people have had to build again after a fire or hurricane or earthquake. We'll manage. It might take ten years, but we'll have things right again."

There were many reasons to be optimistic, they added. Loggers were going back to work. Much of the downed timber was salvageable. The forests would recover. There'd be large-scale replanting. Streams would clear, and fish and wildlife return. Now that folks knew the ash wasn't toxic, they stopped worrying about short-term inhalation during an ashfall. And then roads and bridges would be rebuilt, and homes. Tourists would bolster the stricken economy. Had I heard the latest about the ash? American ceramists wouldn't have to pay $21 for 100 pounds of volcanic ash imported from Italy any more. They could scoop up buckets of the stuff at no cost. St. Helens' ash produced a rich shiny brown glaze on pottery. Maybe someone should start a new business marketing the ash. Anyway you looked at the situation, there'd be jobs for those willing to work.

One state agriculture expert had the misfortune to predict present and future ashfalls would render eastern Washington uninhabitable. He was shouted down. "There's no way farms and orchards are going to die," other experts and growers argued. "They aren't going to die because we won't let them. It's too early to cry havoc. The situation could be a lot different at harvest time."

Actually, growers were immensely cheered in the fall when bumper crops of wheat, hops, and fruit moved to market. Good rainfall in June was thought to be the cause, but studies showed the slight acidity of the ash helped neutralize the alkaline soil and also helped the ground retain water longer.

In setting up a special committee to study long-range effects of the eruptions, Governor Ray stated, "Our people are resilient. There is no defeatist attitude. There's nothing wrong that a lot of money and a little time can't cure." Of course, the Governor meant federally funded assistance. She had sent President Carter a written request after their face-to-face encounter, seeking $2.5 billion to cover the cost of cleanup and recovery from the May eruptions *only.* Not to be outdone, Senator Warren Magnuson declared that he, personally, persuaded Mr. Carter to ask Congress for $860 million to last through September 30, the end of the current fiscal year, and would press for additional appropriations. Both the governor and senator were defeated in November in their bids for reelection, but Congress did appropriate funds to assist the stricken state.

11.

A still Uncertain Future

ighteen days after the May 25 eruption, Mount St. Helens erupted violently on Thursday, June 12. The blast pulverized the lava dome and spewed a substantial plume of steam and ash 50,000 feet into the air for six hours. Pyroclastic flows affected only the uppermost slopes. This time southwestern Washington, including Vancouver, and Portland, Oregon, were inflicted with a one-inch layer of ash. Now, as their waterfront, buildings, beautiful parks, and roads turned gray, Portlanders shared in smaller misery the same experiences as the people of Yakima, Moses Lake, Ritzville, and Spokane, Washington. For a few hours highways and airports were closed and businesses shut down. One reporter wrote, "Now it's our turn to choke on the stuff."

The ashfall loomed catastrophic because Portland's Rose Festival was to open two days later with a grand parade second only to the Pasadena New Year's Day spectacle. Small wonder the residents responded with astonishing energy. They cleaned houses, yards, sidewalks, and even some streets. They helped place sandbags around storm sewers to prevent their becoming clogged, wore facemasks, drove 15-miles-per-hour, and volunteered their help to city and county crews clearing the parade route. The effort paid off, with the Grand Floral Parade stepping out right on schedule.

By June 17 Mount St. Helens had formed a new lava dome about 600 feet wide and 300 feet high. Photographers filmed small fissures on the cooling crust, which geologists said would gape larger as magma oozed up through them in slow, thick flows. However, not enough lava would accumulate to fill the crater and pour down the slopes, like Hawaii's Kilauea, which attracts over two million visitors each year, whether it is resting or erupting. The difference between the two volcanoes was that Kilauea produces lava which flows along the surface, while St. Helens swiftly expels pyroclastic material and steam over a much wider area.

The following Tuesday and Wednesday two sharp seismic blasts were recorded on St. Helens, and steam eruptions attained the 11,000-foot level before drifting southeast without inflicting serious damage. Once again rumors circulated that other volcanic peaks in the Cascades were bound to erupt. Hadn't geological studies proved that in the past several had been active at the same time? Wouldn't this happen again? Now?

Donal Mullineaux, Survey volcanic hazards expert, assured the public that all the Cascade's volcanoes were dormant,

143

except St. Helens. "St. Helens is still in a highly explosive stage. We can expect more large volcanic explosions and pyroclastic flows which could trigger mudslides down onto the valleys below the peak."

Except for building a new dome, the mountain remained quiet for another long spell. Six miles northeast of the summit a Forest Service ecologist found some evidence of "greening up" as salmonberry, a wide variety of ferns, wild currants, huckleberries, skunk cabbage, and buttercups brought color to the ashen slopes. Young trees, especially Pacific silver fir, buried under snowbanks and thus insulated from the pyroclastic flow, were showing healthy tips. The only explosion—a huge one—was in the number of visitors crowding the access roads and Information Centers. Motels and restaurants were jammed and vendors of T-shirts and small packets of "100 percent genuine volcanic ash" enjoyed brisk sales.

Since the mountain wasn't making headlines, reporters followed other leads and turned up unusual stories. One featured Vernon "Bud" Emery, whose name was on the list of missing victims. Toward the end of June he emerged from the woods, very much alive and in good health, with dozens of photographs to prove he had witnessed the May 18 eruption from the Yale Reservoir boat-launching facility southwest of the crater. It had not occurred to him to report his presence to anyone. He had been prospecting for gold and after the ash stopped falling, he continued on his quest, hiking along logging roads and panning in streams not too badly clouded by the eruption. When he returned to Yale to replenish his food supply, he was astounded to learn his name was on the missing list, and promptly took steps to have it removed. When asked if the earth tremors and sulfur-stinking air and noises from the crater and rescue helicopters had disturbed him, he shook his head. Did he find any gold? This time he nodded. "A little. I'm not saying where, but as soon as I can get a permit to go back in the woods, I'll take off again."

Another bit of amusing news was an item reprinted from the July 10 issue of the London *Daily Telegraph*. Adrian Berry, science correspondent, had written, "Cold, wet weather in Britain is probably the result of the volcanic eruptions of Mount St. Helens in the United States. 'The dust emitted by the volcano has merged into a veil covering the northern part of the hemisphere,' said Professor Hubert Lamb, founder of the Climatic Research Unit at the University of East Anglia. 'The quantity of dust emitted by St. Helens could be as great as that which came from the great explosion of Krakatoa in 1883, which caused a noticeable cooling of global weather.' "

Strong disagreement was voiced by Mr. David Houghton, head of the long-term forecasting department at the Meteorological Office at Bracknell. "I don't pretend to be an expert on dust veils, but the atmosphere simply does not behave in the way that Professor Lamb says it does. There is no good scientific reason for attributing the present bad weather to a volcanic eruption."

American readers were not the least upset about the Professor's wrong conclusion because the Weather Service authorities possessed both the facts and satellite photographs to prove that the miniscule amounts of St. Helens' ash in the stratosphere could not possibly alter the weather.

A very different tale originated with the George Platt family of Moses Lake. Barn swallows were building a nest on their property the day several inches of dust sifted down from the May 18 eruption. Normally the birds plastered their nest of straw and twigs with mud scooped up in their beaks. The next day and several following, the busy birds scooped up ash made gluey by light rain. They flew to the nest, worked the tiny portion of mud onto the twigs, flew off and returned quickly with more. Alas! when they plastered wet mud onto the dried layer, it fell off. Trip after trip ended with the same discouraging results. The new mud would not take hold.

The family had noted the swallows' predicament and, while hosing ash off the house and barn, they also carefully cleared a patch of soft ground, exposing the original earth. Driven by their natural desire to complete their nest, the birds once again resumed building. This time the "old" mud served them well. As soon as the nest was finished the female laid four eggs. These hatched July 14 and thrived as their parents stuffed them with insects caught on the wing.

Still another story revealed in a straightforward manner that grasshoppers in eastern Washington's Benton County were having a tough time because of the ash. A U.S. Department of Agriculture survey announced that areas where the grasshopper population density had reached eight pests per square yard in past years now had only from one to three.

Loggers working in swirling dust and householders still shoveling muck from their homes somehow weren't too interested in the swallows' problems or the decline of the grasshopper population in Benton County. They were having more serious problems of their own, having to evacuate speedily on July 22 and again on August 7 when St. Helens produced its fourth and fifth substantial series of ash eruptions accompanied by pyroclastic flows. Possibly the only people excited about these performances were the photographers and tourists. Again the volcano withdrew behind cloud cover to sulk and sputter.

There was one positive note. Both eruptions allowed the Geological Survey and National Weather Service experts to test the flood-warning system installed around the mountain. It worked! Six satellite telemetry stations monitored water amounts and stream flows in the crater and fissures on the outer slopes. As computers flashed suddenly rising figures and the observation plane sighted new activity in the crater, individuals working on the mountain and along the Toutle River were notified, and evacuated well ahead of the moderate flood of muck and debris which spilled down the north slope. While a containment dam being built at Camp Baker 15 miles west of the volcano received some damage, as did some equipment, the heartening news was that the alarm systems worked well. The telemetry systems would work equally during night hours or whenever cloud cover or rains grounded the observation plane. Those factors, plus well-rehearsed evacuation procedures, had paid off. As a teacher employed by the Survey for the summer quipped, "Wait till I tell my students that studying and fire drills really pay off!"

Now an even longer quiet spell set in and people dared hope the mushrooming lava dome would cap the vent so thickly that there would be no more eruptions and St. Helens would drift off to sleep. Road barricades were relaxed, so small communities such as Cougar and others were accessible to residents and hordes of visitors. Only a five-mile area surrounding the ravaged peak remained off-limits to the public. Of course, the peaceful interlude was too good to last. Mount St. Helens still packed nasty surprises. On Thursday, October 16, it erupted from 9:58 to 11:21 P.M., its seventh major eruption. On Friday there were two more separate eruptions, with the plume of steam and ash rising to 47,000 feet. On Saturday it erupted again, the fourth time within forty-eight hours. The newest dome was gone.

By October 25 observers spied still another new one rising around the throat. Geologists announced that the four eruptions were to be counted as one, a single phase. How fortunate there had been four instead of one supereruption! Again the scientists would not, because they could not, predict the duration of the following quiet period nor the approximate date of the next major phase of activity. Regretfully, in spite of all the studies, mapping, graph-making, and statistics gathered, they had learned little applicable to forecasting eruptions. An increasing spate of earthquakes accompanied by harmonic tremors had proved to be not entirely dependable in forecasting. One or the other separately wasn't reliable, either. Changes in the complex gases issuing from the vent gave clues, but would require a great deal more studying. The forecasting done between March 20 and 27 had been based on studies made of Hawaii's Kilauea. But as one scientist remarked, "St. Helens is a different breed of cat. We have to evaluate St. Helens from an entirely new base of evidence." Since no two of St. Helens' eruptions were exactly alike and more were in the offing, there would be no end to the studies or "the homework." At least the alarm systems and evacuation drills had prevented further loss of life.

On November 20, 1980, the Geological Survey issued a report stating that the avalanche triggered by the May 18 eruption had a velocity of 250 miles per hour, nearly twice that estimated earlier. It ranked among the largest in recorded history, displacing 98,000 cubic feet of debris, enough—if the wind had carried it that direction—to bury Portland's business district to the top of the 40-story First National Bank Tower.

The avalanche roared down the north slope in not one but three separate lobes: one devastating the Toutle River valley for 17 miles; a second covering much of Spirit Lake; a third descending the slope, then climbing a 1,000-foot-high ridge before devastating Coldwater Ridge where David Johnston and Reid Blackburn were working and then ravaging the Coldwater Creek drainage. Scientific measurements indicated the total material ejected measured 4.1 cubic kilometers, or about 143,500 cubic feet.

Yet St. Helens was nowhere near the most lethal in history. Mount Vesuvius killed 2,000 people when it buried Pompeii in A.D. 79, and snuffed out 3,000 more lives in a second eruption in 1631. Mount Etna in eastern Sicily exploded in 1669, killing 20,000, but Indonesia's Krakatoa still ranks as the world's most calamitous because its 1883 eruption killed 36,000 people. Even in 1902 Mount Pelée on Martinique Island in the West Indies snuffed out 30,000 lives.

Those who still remain in the St. Helens area are not depressed—*spooked* is the better word—by all they read and hear about St. Helens and other volcanoes in the Cascades and around the world. Most are too occupied learning how to live close by the temperamental and violent peak.

A service station operator at Toutle, interviewed by the author in late October, summed up his and his neighbors' feelings this way. "Remember years ago when one of the big oil companies advertised its gasoline was like having a tiger in your gas tank? That's what we got here, only the tiger is St. Helens and it's out in the backyard. No one is kidding us about the danger, and we're not kidding ourselves.

Nobody on earth can crack a whip over that crater and make it behave. These science fellows are all excited about St. Helens being a living laboratory but you don't see 'em buying homes and settling here.

"They say this place will be as famous as Old Faithful in Yellowstone Park, or the Grand Canyon. Well, we'll live with that, too. Some days it's like Grand Central station around here. These tourists are something—parking in our driveways, dumping litter on our streets, treating us 'mountain folk,' they call us, like hillbillies. Soon as the rains come, they'll be gone. We'll stay, and we'll cope with whatever St. Helens throws at us. We'll manage, and our kids, and their kids. We have to and they'll have to if they want to live in this beautiful country because one thing for dang sure, Mount St. Helens is going to be here long, long after we're all gone."

In January, 1981, Mount St. Helens puffed steam on several occasions and twitched with subterranean microquakes. Area residents merely shrugged. When persistent newspaper reporters pressed USGS scientists for a forecast, one, a young woman geologist, pretty much summed up the situation by saying, "While we feel the potential of a major eruption is way down, there is still a chance of a small pop which probably would not have effects outside the crater. Although the dome remains unstable, we probably will not have any sort of major blowout." Then she smiled and reminded the reporters, "It's always up to the mountain, so we can never be absolutely certain what may happen."

The author's service station operator friend agreed. "Sure, it's up to the mountain. Always has been. Always will be."

Additional materials

A great deal has been written about Mount St. Helens since it erupted on May 18, 1980. Newspapers and magazines have given it full coverage, and at least a dozen books have been published. An active volcano right at home is something people want to know about.

The materials listed below are available. The printed matter is distributed free of charge; there is a fee for the photographs. Address requests to:

Gifford Pinchot National Forest
Pacific Northwest Region
500 West 12th Street
Vancouver, WA 98660

MOUNT ST. HELENS

A six-page magazine-format brochure in color featuring excellent photographs, maps, charts, and brief diary of eruptions. Also available at Visitor Centers in Washington.

MOUNT ST. HELENS GEOLOGICAL AREA VOLCANO INFORMATION

Fact Sheet—August 8, 1980. Background information, current activity, losses, potential hazards, and chronology of events through August 7.

MOUNT ST. HELENS INFORMATION MAP

One sheet, black-and-white. Shows location of the volcano in relation to surrounding communities, Visitor Centers on I-5 freeway, Vancouver, Portland, the Columbia River, as well as other viewpoints and camping grounds.

ERUPTIONS OF MOUNT ST. HELENS

One sheet, black-and white. Prehistoric, historic, and present eruptions in concise text.

FOREST SERVICE NEWS—Recreation Report, October 1, 1980

Five pages. Information on Visitor Information sites, St. Helens Ranger Districts and woodcutting permits needed, campgrounds and picnic areas open, hunting zones open and closed, locations to gather mushrooms or berries, improved trails. Essential for recreation use. Seasonal updated releases must be requested for spring, summer, and fall use in 1981 and later.

VOLCANIC ASHFALL

How to prepare for and what to do during a volcanic ashfall. Six-page brochure. Also available from:

Federal Emergency Management Agency
Region X
Federal Regional Center
Bothell, WA 98011

MOUNT ST. HELENS PHOTOS AVAILABLE FOR PURCHASE

Write for free listing describing 9" x 9" black-and-white photographs at a cost of $3 each, and also available in larger sizes, as well as two rolls of microfilm. Address request to:

EROS Data Center
U. S. Geological Survey
Sioux Falls, SD 57198

Index

MARIAN T. PLACE, the author of over forty books for children and young people, specializes in the American West and is the recipient of four Golden Spur Awards given by the Western Writers of America for Best Western juvenile novel and Best Western juvenile nonfiction title. She has worked as a newspaperwoman and a children's librarian, and has published over two hundred articles. Her first book about North America's monster, *On the Track of Bigfoot,* won the 1977 Garden State Children's Book Award.

She and her husband camped and hiked the Mount St. Helens area many times and researched the volcano disaster area by car and plane between June and late October following the 1980 eruptions. Winter residents of Arizona, their summer home is at Bend, Oregon, close by Mount Bachelor and Three Sisters volcanoes and the million-visitor Lava Lands Center.